# A LIFE WOVEN IN Love

A Fresh, Bible-Based
Perspective on Discipleship:
Weaving a Life of Faith
Expressing Itself
Through Love

Jacqueline East

Ark House Press
arkhousepress.com

© 2025 Jacqueline East | First Edition

All rights reserved. No part of this publication may be reproduced, stored, or transmitted in any form or by any means, electronic, mechanical, photocopying, recording, scanning, or otherwise without written permission from the publisher. It is illegal to copy this book, post it to a website, or distribute it by any other means without permission.

Whilst AI was used in the creation of the book cover and images in this book, no AI has been used in the creation of any written content.

Scriptures taken from the Holy Bible, New International Version®, NIV®. Copyright © 1973, 1978, 1984, 2011 by Biblica, Inc.™ Used by permission of Zondervan. All rights reserved worldwide. www.zondervan.com. The "NIV" and "New International Version" are trademarks registered in the United States Patent and Trademark Office by Biblica, Inc.™

Cataloguing in Publication Data:
Title: A Life Woven In Love
ISBN: 978-1-7641362-5-9 (pbk)
Subjects: REL012050  RELIGION / Christian Living / Love & Marriage; REL012040  RELIGION / Christian Living / Inspirational; REL012120  RELIGION / Christian Living / Spiritual Growth.

A copy of this book has been sent to the National Library of Australia and State Library of New South Wales.

# CONTENTS

Acknowledgement of Country..................................................................ix
Personal Acknowledgements..................................................................xi
Introduction........................................................................................ xiii

## Part 1
### The Bridegroom

The Bridegroom's Woven Blanket - Scene 1 ............................................ 3
Chapter 1: The Bridegroom .................................................................... 4
Chapter 2: Re-Thinking About Thinking ................................................ 9
Chapter 3: Commitment, Communion, And Celebration..................... 14

## Part 2
### The Mud

The Bridegroom's Woven Blanket - Scene 2 .......................................... 23
Chapter 4: The Problem With The Mud............................................... 26
Chapter 5: The Beginning Of Unions.................................................... 32
Chapter 6: The Wedding Planner's Attitude ......................................... 38

## Part 3
## The Blanket

The Bridegroom's Woven Blanket - Scene 3 ............................................. 47
Chapter 7: Blankets Of Love – Handwoven By Jesus ...................... 50
Chapter 8: Our Uniquely Personalised Blankets ............................... 56
Chapter 9: Dealing With Our Own Muddy Mess ............................ 63

## Part 4
## The Threads Of Love

The Bridegroom's Woven Blanket - Scene 4 ............................................. 75
Chapter 10: Representations Of Love .................................................. 77
Chapter 11: An Invitation To Love ...................................................... 81
Chapter 12: Offering Someone A Blanket Of Love ........................... 88

## Part 5
## The Partnership

The Bridegroom's Woven Blanket - Scene 5 ............................................. 99
Chapter 13: Covering Or Smothering ................................................ 102
Chapter 14: An Intimate Partnership ................................................. 113
Chapter 15: A Blanket Of Healing ...................................................... 124

## Part 6
## Flourishing Communities woven in LOVE

The Bridegroom's Woven Blanket - Scene 6 ............................................. 135
Chapter 16: Communities Woven In Love ......................................... 138

Chapter 17: Truth Woven In Love ........................................................ 147
Chapter 18: United In Christ, Connected With Each Other ............. 155
Conclusion: Dancing in the Mud ........................................................ 163
A Prayer ................................................................................................. 165

## Part 7
## FINAL COMMENTS

A Vision of Community ...................................................................... 169
The Bridegroom's Woven Blanket - The Compiled Story ................... 175
Support Resources for those who have suffered trauma ..................... 189
Also By Jacqueline East ........................................................................ 191
About the Author ................................................................................. 193

To my church community at Hamilton,
You embody grace, inclusion, and love.
Thank you for following Jesus so faithfully
and for providing a safe space
to freely discover him, worship him, and love him
with integrity and authenticity.

And

To Andrew and Felicity,
Congratulations!
May the life of love you weave
fill your hearts and bring you ever-increasing joy.

# ACKNOWLEDGEMENT OF COUNTRY

I would like to acknowledge the original
custodians of this beautiful land
on which I have the privilege to live, write, and work.
I pay my respects to the Worimi people,
and to their elders past and present.

I also pay my respects to the Awabakal people and their elders
on whose land I worship with my church
family at Hamilton Baptist Church.

am grateful for the First Nations' people who have nurtured this land of Australia with wisdom and stewardship for countless generations. I recognise that this care is ongoing, and I pray that we will commit to listening, learning, and working together to ensure that we protect and preserve the land for future generations. May we walk forward in respect, reciprocity, and a shared dedication to the wellbeing of this country and all who call it home.

For those people who have suffered division, trauma, heartache, and brokenness, I pray for God's healing, restoration, justice, and grace. I am deeply sorry for the wrongdoings to First Nations' people in our fractured history and ask for God's forgiveness over our country and its people. May his Spirit bring us to a place where we can move forward as a united nation with a collaborative heart, wrapped in his woven blanket of love.

# PERSONAL ACKNOWLEDGEMENTS

I want to say a huge thank you
to the beautiful congregation of Hamilton Baptist Church
for your contribution to this book.
Our discussions as a church have informed its content
and your love as a family has infused every page.

I extend enormous thanks to:
Sergio Nuñez for your graphic design collaboration with images,
Kate Olivia for your photographic expertise,
Mike Hocking-Gill for your proofreading,
James Cox for your insights and editorial comments,
Joy Herron for your labour of love in extensive editing,
and to Felicity Fairley for believing in this project and
providing vision that shaped its formation.

I offer a warm thank you to the superb team at Ark House Press
for making this dream a reality and sharing my work with the world.

And to Jesus, our bridegroom, you are the focus of our lives
and the heartbeat of our mission.
Thank you for showing us how to weave a life of love together.

# INTRODUCTION

Have you ever wondered what you're here for?

"What's the purpose of it all?" you may ask.

That's the quintessential question people have been trying to answer since the beginning of humanity. What are we here for? Christianity offers an answer: to love and be loved. On that, I believe most Christians agree. Yet the outworking of love is complicated, messy, and feels like we're trudging through mud. What Jesus does is offer a solution. His solution doesn't take away all our problems, but allows us to grow through them, learn from them, become people whose faith is strengthened by them, and whose character is shaped by them. Jesus helps us weave a unique expression of love into the fabric of our lives as we learn to offer who we are and what we have – in the middle of the muckiness of life – to serve one another.

I gracefully offer this book to you as a fresh viewpoint on what love looks like: a hand-woven, personalised blanket, crafted by Jesus, the bridegroom. This idea is encapsulated by the metaphor embedded in this book titled 'The Bridegroom's Woven Blanket'. It originates from a heart that is absolutely devoted to Jesus. It is published to offer fresh perspective and hope for the future, not as a means of criticism or judgement on how things have been done in the past. It is written from the lens of my faith which is continually evolving in its understanding and is becoming more wholesome and helpful.

My prayer for the church of Jesus is that we may be inspired to keep envisioning a bright, optimistic, eternal future that starts in our hearts and homes today. I pray that we, as his family of faith, will be motivated to embrace its mission with vitality, creating restorative communities of faith that embody Jesus' love.

I also wholeheartedly pray that you will gain a deeper appreciation of the work of Jesus and what it means to partner with him, empowered by his Holy Spirit. May you be strengthened in hope, inspired by love, and motivated through faith. And may you keep believing in the goodness of people and the healing power of Jesus, even if you've seen and experienced the damaging effects of the imperfections of our collective humanness in the church. If you have been hurt by the institution of religion or by Christians, please, please… I implore you. Don't give up. Jesus' healing is available. The way religion has expressed itself in the past can inform how to do things more beneficially in the future. There is a way of re-thinking discipleship which can launch us into a faith-fuelled future, with endless possibilities that can lovingly and gracefully transform our world.

My hope is that God's Holy Spirit will stoke the fires of your heart and stir something in you that will ignite a spark of excitement and anticipation as you read these pages. May he kindle in you a desire to love Jesus more passionately, to live more purposefully, and offer yourself more freely as you re-discover what it means to weave a life of faith expressing itself in love in this mucky, messy, yet stunningly glorious, journey of life.

With love,
*Jackie*

# *Part 1*
# THE BRIDEGROOM

# THE BRIDEGROOM'S WOVEN BLANKET

*Scene 1*

Picture a beautiful bride. It's the day of her wedding. She's dressed in a long, white wedding gown that fits her perfectly. Her hair is done up and not a strand is out of place. She looks resplendent from head to toe. She is absolutely spotless. She's totally gorgeous. She's prepared. She's ready.

The limousine comes to pick her up to take her to the church where her future husband awaits.

"Congratulations, Ma'am," the chauffeur says as he opens the door for her.

"Thank you!" she replies excitedly as she takes her seat.

They set off. The bride can feel butterflies in her tummy as she spots the church in the distance, knowing her future husband is there waiting for her…

## Chapter 1

# THE BRIDEGROOM

Most of us love a good wedding. Even if it's not for the ceremony or that breathtaking moment when the bride enters the room and everyone stands in awe, at least we get to catch up with friends or meet new people… and there's cake. Right? Who doesn't like cake? We go (hopefully) because we love and support the couple getting married, praying for the most perfect and happiest of days for the blossoming pair, but sometimes things go a little pear-shaped.

When it comes to weddings, we've come to expect the unexpected. We have our cameras at the ready to capture those wedding bloopers. Who knows what might happen? There could be mishaps or disasters like wardrobe malfunctions, uncooperative flower girls, slip ups and trip ups, messed up vows, terrible speeches, crazy dancing under the influence, or cake disasters. Our phones are on, ready for the snapshot of the century.

This book began as a series of four messages I presented in church inspired by the wedding of our pastor and his beautiful bride. Our church community had been involved in most aspects of the wedding from wardrobe advice to catering, from setting up the event on a property belonging to a couple in our church, to the decorating. That's where I was involved. The day had gone smoothly, the ceremony was lovely, and the setting was stunning, if I don't say so myself. There were birds chirping in the background and wedge-tailed eagles flying overhead. We were moved by the vows of commitment the bride and groom made to each other. We relished the sense of communion of the occasion; the unity we felt in being together. We had fun celebrating and savouring the delectable catering. But is a wedding really a wedding without mishaps? The music not coming on quite on cue, the heat of the morning where one guest collapsed, followed by twenty minutes of bucketing rain that soaked everything, leaving a collapsed gazebo, rumbling thunder, and flashes of lightning during the speeches. The lesson: no matter how well planned the wedding is, expect the unexpected.

Weddings are something people can easily identify with. They are a significant part of world-cultural events. Whilst they are celebrated differently around the globe, most people have been to a wedding at some stage in their lives and would be able to identify the bride and groom.

One of the unexpected announcements we discover early in Jesus' ministry is that he identifies himself as a bridegroom. It is a prominent recount, found in all three synoptic gospels. (Mark 2:19, Matthew 9:15 & Luke 5:35) Before I continue, I would like to note that sadly there have been many cheesy things said about the concept of Jesus being the husband of his bride, the church. I sincerely hope that this is not one of them! I tiptoe into this analogy lightly…

When Jesus made this symbolic representation of himself as the bridegroom, we can assume that his audience would have been aware of what that culturally signified, but I'm sure they would have left scratching their heads, puzzled by the context Jesus used. Let's read the passage from Mark and I'll explain...

> **Mark 2:18-22:** "Now John's disciples and the Pharisees were fasting. Some people came and asked Jesus, '"How is it that John's disciples and the disciples of the Pharisees are fasting, but yours are not?'" Jesus answered, '"How can the guests of the bridegroom fast whilst he is with them? They cannot, so long as they have him with them. But the time will come when the bridegroom will be taken from them, and on that day they will fast.
>
> No one sews a patch of unshrunk cloth on an old garment. Otherwise, the new piece will pull away from the old, making the tear worse. And no one pours new wine into old wineskins. Otherwise, the wine will burst the skins, and both the wine and the wineskins will be ruined. No, they pour new wine into new wineskins.'"

The historical context is that John the Baptist had been imprisoned (Mark 1:14) and Jesus had begun his public ministry. People started to take notice and asked him why his disciples were doing things differently to John's disciples and the Pharisees. Why were the others fasting, but his weren't? Sounds like a simple question. They wanted clarity, yet Jesus provided them with a cloudy answer.

They were asking him, "Why is this going on?" Possibly with an implied, "And what are *you* going to do about it?" Or potentially a condescending, "Why are you allowing this divergence from the norm?" In short, the question seems to imply, "Why are you teaching your disciples to *not* do something they are *supposed* to do?"

# THE BRIDEGROOM

In Mark 2:19-20 Jesus answered, "I am the bridegroom. The guests of a bridegroom don't need to fast whilst he's with them. One day the bridegroom will not be here, and they'll fast then." *(Paraphrased)* In this was the implication that he was the bridegroom and, as his disciples were his guests, they didn't need to fast whilst he was with them. To our knowledge, Jesus didn't explain that thought any further. He simply left them pondering.

To add another puzzling idea to that already strange response to the question on fasting, Jesus added the concept of sewing unshrunk cloth onto an old garment and pouring new wine into old wineskins. If they weren't scratching their heads in the beginning, they'd be scratching now.

What did he mean?

What Jesus was referring to about the cloth and wineskin, was that there is an inconsistency, an incompatibility, about taking something new and putting it in something old. With the wineskins, putting new wine in old wineskins can break the whole shebang! The tear can worsen, the wineskins can burst and then we're left with nothing! What we need is to put something new into something new. The interpretation: For the people to understand what Jesus meant about being the bridegroom, they were going to have to re-think. They were going to need an openness of mind to form a new way of thinking. That's not easy.

Over the next three years, Jesus goes on, not just teaching the people about the kingdom of God but teaching them *how to think*. That is the skill of an excellent teacher. A good teacher will tell you content, teach you how to understand it, and help you learn it and apply it. A GREAT teacher, like Jesus, teaches people how to think about thinking; how to look at what they know, see it from a fresh perspective, and come to a new understanding of how it applies to their lives. Jesus taught people to re-think what the kingdom of God was, then he showed them a whole new way of doing church and life in relationship with God and one another. When we look at this wider picture, all we can do is marvel at his teaching prowess and go, "WOW."

Let's take a closer look at the process of re-thinking about thinking.

## Chapter 2
# RE-THINKING ABOUT THINKING

like the book of Mark. It is action-packed. Mark dives into his narrative with John the Baptist preparing the way for Jesus, which gives the context for Jesus' baptism. Jesus then goes into the wilderness and is tempted. Then John is put in prison… All this leads up to Jesus' first big announcement in Mark 1:15. (All that in fourteen verses! I told you he was fast!)

> **Mark 1:15:** "The time has come," he said. "The kingdom of God has come near. Repent and believe the good news!"
>
> **Repent** and **believe**. Two key words.

Repenting is re-thinking what we know. The word repent comes from the Latin 're', meaning to go back again, and the word 'pent' which comes from the Latin word 'pensare' which means 'to think'. So, repent simply means to go back and think about something, i.e. 're-think' it. When Jesus said, "Repent and believe the good news" he was inviting his listeners to re-think their ideas of the kingdom of God so they could take on board the new information he was going to give them and then believe it deeply. The beliefs we hold inform our actions. If they change, then our behaviour, habits, and attitudes can change and become part of our new lifestyle. To be concise: how we think determines our lives.

J.K. Rowling, literary genius that she is, came up with a brilliant way of looking at the idea of re-thinking in the Harry Potter series. (Let me make it clear. I'm not promoting magic in church, ok? Rather, I'm drawing on the imaginative expertise of a brilliant writer who posed a left-field way of looking at this idea of thinking. Got it?)

The clever concept she came up with in Hogwarts School of Magic was the idea of a 'pensieve'. J.K. Rowland took the word 'pensare' and added it to the word 'sieve,' which is a container or receptacle. In other words, she created a vessel in which to put thoughts and memories. In the movie series, the pensieve looks a lot like an infant baptismal font you'd find in an old, stone church building. I thought this was curious because baptism uses the same concept. When we are baptised, we go into the water taking the 'old us' and symbolically dying to it, then come out changed - someone new - embracing the resurrected life we have in Christ. (2 Corinthians 5:17) We begin a new way of life, in line with our new way of thinking, which is based on trusting God (i.e. faith).

In the case of the pensieve, the wizard would extract a thought or memory from their mind with the aid of their wand and place it into the water to be magically transported into it, allowing the viewer to see the image from different perspectives, varied angles, and in diverse ways. This allowed them to investigate the individual associated with the memory, permitting the viewer to understand how that person became who they became, and hence did what they did. In the book series, one of the main uses for the pensieve was to understand what the enemy, Voldemort, was like as a child as Tom Riddle; how he used to think, and how he became the deadly evil he became.

In summary, they took an old thought, viewed it from different perspectives and came out with fresh understanding. It's a lot like that with us. If we look back at our memories, we can see who we were and how we used to think. That process helps us understand how we became the person that we are today. It's a marvellous way of thinking about thinking.

So how do we re-think what we know about scripture? Great question! One way is to look at a particular passage and try and think back to when we began to understand that part of the Bible. Put the passage in the pensieve, so to speak. How old were we? What was our life like back then? Who were the main people influencing our point of view? What were they teaching? What books were we reading? What audio-digital material were we absorbing? What did that understanding tell us about ourselves and our relationship with God? What did we do with that information? How did it play out in our decisions and, consequently, our lives? Why not take a passage of scripture and just have a go? See what comes up for you.

Jesus spent three years teaching his followers how to re-think. He challenged his listeners to examine their beliefs from perspectives they hadn't conceived of. He used a wide range of images like family, light, vines, doors, coins, baptism, weddings, funerals, sheep, farming, bread… The list goes on… and on. Jesus communicated in pictures, using common things that people understood, then he took those images and either added to their meaning, explained their meaning, or redefined their meaning, depending on what he was trying to do with the symbol.

Pictures weren't his only tools. In fact, he had a whole range of tools in his toolbox to pull out and effectively use for each situation. Here are some examples of the types of tools he used.

- Comparisons, like saying, "What is easier… this… or *this*?"
- Answering questions with questions
- Changing the meaning of commonly understood themes
- Repetition of ideas using different illustrations
- Being a role model; he practiced what he preached
- Use of spontaneous events as teaching opportunities
- Lists of things
- Powerful storytelling
- Parables
- Metaphors
- Lots of examples
- Incorporation of Old Testament scriptures
- Practical instructions
- Rhetorical questions
- Wise use of prophecy and words of knowledge
- And many others…

One of the things I love about the way Jesus taught most was that he allowed people to make up their own minds in choosing how to implement his teaching. His manner wasn't imposing, nor did he follow people up and question them in how they were carrying out his teaching. He just let them do whatever they needed to do in response to how he taught. He let them simmer over what he was teaching and then apply it. He presented a new way of thinking and allowed those thoughts to embed themselves into their everyday lives. It was such a gracious approach.

Through the content and methods Jesus used to teach he was helping his followers develop a new understanding of the kingdom of God. In effect, the methods he used helped them to deconstruct their current understanding of faith and reconstruct it in a way that was more aligned with God's heart and purpose.

"The kingdom of God is near," Jesus announced at the beginning of his ministry. As he embodied the nature and the values of the kingdom of God, he allowed his disciples to see first-hand what the kingdom was like and how to live it. By living alongside them, he infused their lives with the character and values of God. As he did, Jesus helped them to re-think what it was all about.

When we spend time with Jesus, through prayer, worship, studying the Bible, or other means, the same thing happens to us. His Holy Spirit changes us to align us with the character of God and the values of his kingdom, bringing our hearts and minds in aligned agreement with his. We, little by little, are being transformed. This happens through repentance, because God is kind enough to not want to leave us in the mucky state we're in, instead he helps us to continually renew our thoughts and live more abundant, victorious lives. (Romans 2:4, John 10:10b)

It's a lot like when we spend a significant portion of time with someone we love, like a blossoming couple wanting to get married. Let's explore some themes that emerge from that picture.

# Chapter 3

# COMMITMENT, COMMUNION, AND CELEBRATION

We love a good wedding, right? The ceremony and the vows often require a tissue at the ready. We see the couple wanting to create a life together and strengthen their union by making a formal declaration of that commitment. There are witnesses, often friends and family, who love and support them and choose to celebrate their decision to dedicate their lives to one another, for life.

I'm wondering if you can see some themes emerging from the image of marriage.

The main themes I can readily identify are commitment, communion, and celebration. Let me expand on these themes using Jesus' representation of himself to the public by calling himself a bridegroom.

Jesus was dedicating himself to his disciples through his commitment to them. I believe this commitment was saying, "As the bridegroom I am right here, and I am dedicated to you. I'm not going anywhere. I'm going to teach you all you need to know, help you re-think your thinking, and show you a new way to live. I am totally, one hundred percent, absolutely, no-questions-asked, committed to this." That same commitment he had to his disciples when he walked this earth is the same dedication he has to us today.

I don't think it will ever be possible for any of us to completely understand the level of commitment Jesus has towards us. His commitment meant leaving his Father (parent-figure) in heaven to become a human being, giving up his 'God-ness' - his omnipresence (being always everywhere), omniscience (being all knowing), and omnipotence (being all powerful) - to become one of us *for all eternity*. That's a *massive* commitment!

I'll pause for a moment to let that sink in…

In identifying as a bridegroom, Jesus was also confirming his desire to commune with his disciples and to form a united partnership, a bonded family of faith.

As we saw earlier, Jesus' identification as a bridegroom was in response to a question posed to him about fasting. Fasting is a type of ritual where people set aside time to be with God (or 'commune' with him). The people asking Jesus the question about fasting may have been challenging him, possibly unsettled that Jesus may have been encouraging his followers *not* to commune with God through fasting. They may have been pointing a finger at him, accusing him of disregarding customs and traditions, implying that the way he was teaching his disciples was *wrong* (whereas John's disciples and the Pharisees were doing it *right*.) Regardless of their motives, Jesus' response cut through the heart of their question with an unexpected answer that was left-field, ambiguous, and caused them to stop and think. There was a reason why his disciples didn't need to fast. Wasn't it obvious? He was the bridegroom. His disciples were the guests. As his guests, they didn't need to fast whilst the bridegroom was with them. Full stop. Clear as crystal? Hmmm. Probably not.

Fasting and prayer are intrinsically linked. They are activities Christians refer to as spiritual disciplines; things we do to help build and strengthen our relationship with God. Usually when people fast, they are praying about something specific, like searching for an answer from God, asking God to intervene in a particular circumstance, or praying for God to help a loved one…

For me, fasting isn't just about answers to my prayers, because a lot of the time I haven't seen those answers. It's about my relationship with God. It's about communion. Carving out time to spend with God, wanting to hear from him, or see him move in some way, has always brought about a level of connection with him that I don't normally experience outside of that space. The process does something transformative in my heart.

Prayer is all about our heart alignment with God's. When we set aside time to dedicate it to cultivating our *union with* God (that's what communion means: with unity) we allow ourselves to be more open to his transformative work in our lives. Most often, I've found that through prayer and fasting the circumstances I'm praying for may not have changed, but my perspective, attitude, and understanding have. It has been a time of reflecting deeply, giving my heart and mind time to re-think. *I* change in the process.

When we commit time to seeking God's heart, mind, and purposes for a situation something happens to us in the process of communing with him. We draw closer to him. We open our hearts to seek *his* will, rather than our own. We grow in the depth of our understanding of God's character and appreciate the values of his kingdom as they outwork themselves in our daily lives. We become more united with him. By dedicating time to spend with God, and even simply acknowledging him throughout our day, we are building our union with Jesus and strengthening the relationship we have with him; being more aligned with him.

When Jesus is found discouraging his disciples from fasting, it makes sense that people were alarmed. Teachers were meant to encourage people to draw near to God through prayer and fasting, not *abstain* from it. Yet Jesus, through his controversial methods, was communicating something very profound.

We have the benefit of hindsight in reading and interpreting scripture. We get to ponder Biblical accounts and derive meaning from what *may* have been said at the time. In this case, I feel like Jesus was saying to his disciples, "Those people over there, they can fast, but you don't need to because I'm right here! Any of those questions that you have that you would have been fasting about just ask *me*! I represent God. (Hebrews 1:3a) I appreciate that you don't understand what I'm saying now but I'm going to be here, in an intimate space of connection and communion with you, until the end. Ok. Yes, there's going to be an end. A time will come when I'm not going to be personally available to you anymore, but until that point, you can ask me whatever you want. You don't need to desperately seek, pray, and fast for answers from God because *I am right here*! I AM God, Emmanuel, in the flesh, with you. (Matthew 1:23) Let's celebrate this time together whilst we can."

This representation of Jesus as the bridegroom was an invitation to those who would follow Jesus to be intimately connected with him. He was inviting them to get to know him. He was inviting them to live life with them. He was inviting them with welcoming, open arms to share their hearts, dreams, problems, uncertainties, questions, paradoxes, hopes, and ideas with him. He was inviting them to be united with him and align their hearts with God's, because he – himself – was God incarnate. They didn't need to look any further. God was present in their midst. (John 1:14)

The disciples in Jesus' day were privileged to walk with him, talk, pray, and eat with him, minister with him, laugh, sing, and cry with him, and learn from him. It was a unique time in history. For approximately three years they were able to know Jesus intimately and allow his life to infuse theirs, his words to sharpen their minds, and his love to govern their decisions. I'm sure it would have been a season of the deepest, richest celebration of life in the history of humankind on earth.

Yet somehow, in Jesus' eyes, those who haven't seen him are more blessed than the disciples who were with Jesus at the time.

> **John 20:29:** "Then Jesus told him, '"Because you have seen me, you have believed; blessed are those who have not seen and yet have believed.'"

Why are we blessed? It has something to do with faith. In not seeing, yet still believing, our faith is stronger. It requires faith to believe that Jesus is still powerfully present, intervening on our behalf, concerned about our lives, lovingly caring for our circumstances, and somehow outworking the billions of good, bad, and downright ugly details of our lives in our favour. (Romans 8:28) In the process, we grow in our faith, strengthen our hearts, and cultivate his character in us – even though we can't see him.

Jesus still invites us to follow him. He is holding out his arms, welcoming us into a world of meaning, revelation, exploration, vulnerability, intimacy, and wisdom wrapped in unfathomable, unconditional love. He invites us into a safe world of discovery, where no question is too big or too small, where no hurt is too painful, or sin is too disdainful. It is a world where we can come – just as we are – and live life with him in a beautiful union of our spirits (not dissimilar to an engagement). Isn't that something worthy of celebration? We can celebrate the unity we can have with him. We can celebrate the commitment he has displayed to us and continues to manifest through his faithfulness to us. He is truly wonderful. He chose to celebrate his life with us. Will you accept his invitation to celebrate life with *him*?

Allow me to ask you some personal questions. Is your faith something you celebrate? How do you celebrate your life with Jesus? What sparks your heart of delight and passion for him? What gets you excited about living your life with him? Did you know that he takes great delight in *YOU*? (Zephaniah 3:17)

If you find the idea about being passionate about a relationship with Jesus challenging, can I assure you that I get it. I appreciate how hard it is to be ardently 'on fire' about Jesus all the time, particularly when you've been hurt by the church, wounded by people who profess to love him. I do. I truly do. I have been profoundly hurt by Christians who love Jesus. I also know that in my imperfection, I too have hurt others and for that I am truly sorry. I am incapable of following Jesus and acting in love all the time. This is where grace and forgiveness are so important. All I can do is point to the one who is perfect, who is unfailing love, and whose mercy is greater than all my failures. He is the one we follow, despite how we stumble and fall in the mud of life.

Christians are very, very imperfect representations of Jesus in this world, yet Jesus has never stopped loving you. He has never stopped caring about you. He knows your hurts and heartbreaks. He holds your tears and embraces your pain. Through it all he invites you to be held, to rest in his arms, to feel his love and know, truly know – deep down in your gut kind of knowing – that he will never give up on you. His healing is available to you and his compassion and kindness can restore your soul.

Jesus offers himself as a loving husband to a church that desperately needs him. He wants to partner with her. He wants to cherish her and will devote himself to her for all the ages of existence to come.

That is the kind of husband the bride in our story was waiting to marry. That's why she had butterflies in her tummy. She couldn't wait to get to the church to begin their new life together.

But something was about to happen that would stop her in her tracks. The seams of the story are about to tear…

Something went ka-thunk.

# Part 2
## THE MUD

# THE BRIDEGROOM'S WOVEN BLANKET

*Scene 2*

Riding comfortably in the limo, the bride smiles to herself, picturing her husband waiting for her at the church.

Unfortunately, the beautiful image she envisioned is suddenly jolted from her mind by the sound of loud splutter ka-thunk of the engine as the limo shudders to a halt, breaking down. Despite the bride's attempt to will the car into motion it refuses to budge any further.

The limo driver turns to the bride and says, "I'm sorry ma'am. You'll have to walk."

He gets out of the car and opens the door for her. She steps out, but her beautiful white shoe lands in a puddle of mud.

The driver highlights her predicament. "Sorry, ma'am," he apologises. "It's like that *all* the way."

The bride looks up from her muddied shoe to view the panorama. As far as she can see there is mud. It's an impossibly big, swamp-like puddle. She realises that she can't go around it. It's too far. There's no helicopter to fly her over it. She's just going to have to walk *through* it.

In her heart, the bride knows there is no other place in the world she wants to be. Her husband and the life she longs to build with him are there, waiting for her; so close, and yet so… far… away. She steps out. She puts her foot boldly into the mud, hoping to clean her shoes when she reaches the other side.

The bride is determined. She starts to walk, yet the more steps she takes she realises that the mud is a LOT deeper and a LOT harder to move through than she expected. At first, the hem of her dress gets dirty. Then she finds that the mud is reaching up to her knees and she's straining to push her way through it. She keeps moving forward. She's *got* to get there. But just when she thinks the worst is over, she falls, headfirst. She tears her dress and is covered in filth.

By the time the bride reaches the steps of the church she's a complete mess…

Unexpectedly, the bride is greeted by a lovely, experienced, neatly dressed wedding planner who says to her, "Oh my! Deary me! You've been through a bit of muck, haven't you?" (For some reason she has a British accent.) "Dry your tears, love. It will be *all* right."

The bride wipes her eyes with her hands but is interrupted by the wedding planner.

"Ohhh. Best not, pet. Now you've got more mud on your face. Shame, that." She clicks her tongue.

"What am I supposed to do?" the bride cries out.

"Don't you worry about a thing, love," the planner consoles. "I've got something here that will make everything *perfect*."

She unzips a little purse buckled around her waist where she keeps all her bits and bobs for bridal emergencies and pulls out a beautiful, handsized piece of white, satin fabric.

"Here we are, dear. This will do *just* the trick."

The bride stares at her with a puzzled look.

The wedding planner gets out some pins and fastens the piece of fabric on to the tear on her dress. Then she stands back and admires her work, looking at her little patch of white satin, yet ignoring the fact that the pins are beginning to rip the dress and that blobs of mud are starting to seep through from the dress, staining the little piece of material.

"Ah! My work is done. You can go in now, love. Off you go dear, spit spot."

Zipping up her little purse, the wedding planner departs.

The bride is left on the steps of the church in utter disbelief. The patch of material cannot fix the tear or cover the mud. She doesn't know what to do. Worst still, she's so embarrassed and ashamed of the state of her dress and the muck all over her that she doesn't dare go through the doors of the church to face her husband who is waiting inside. All she can do is fall on the steps, bury her face in her hands, and cry…

# Chapter 4
# THE PROBLEM WITH THE MUD

Ka-thunk. Things broke down. The plan unravelled. The complication of the story emerged. The plot thickened.

Taking one step out of the pristine limo, the bride was immediately and irrevocably tainted by the mud. She had no other option. If she wanted to attain her heart's desire and be united with her husband, she had to step into the mud and begin to trudge.

Does it feel like that to you? Does walking through this life feel like trudging? Countless times throughout my life I've found myself exasperatedly crying out, "Why does everything have to be so ***difficult***?" It's because we have a problem with mud.

If you haven't realised it yet, the mud represents the sin in the world. We have a problem with sin. I don't like to call it that because it sounds very religious and point-the-finger-y. Nevertheless, it's the universal word we use to describe the state of our hearts and the state of our world that is tarnished by our lack of trust in God. (Romans 14:23b) Every time we choose to act in contra to the values of God's kingdom and the character of his heart we sin. Yes. We have the freedom as human beings to act in accordance with our own will and values. The condition of that freedom is that we must live with the consequences of those choices. That's where things get mucky.

Every choice we make has consequences. Our lives come into formation by the billions of choices we make; the things we think, say, and do. All these choices are determined by what is in our hearts – what we believe and what we value. When God looks at us, he doesn't look at the external. He looks at our hearts and what is *motivating* the things we do. (1 Samuel 16:7b)

Because we choose our own 'modus operandi', essentially doing things our own way, we have the fun privilege of having to figure out how to live with the repercussions of those decisions not only for ourselves, but in relationship with everyone else in the world who is operating the same way. That creates a LOT of mud. Fun, fun, FUN! (That 'fun' was sarcasm, just to be clear!)

Take one example from your own life. It could be something very simple, like something you may have said to your partner, friend, or work colleague. It could be something you did to a family member – whether accidentally or on purpose. It could even be something you failed to do or something you didn't say that caused a problem. Regardless of what it was, stop and consider the fallout. What were the consequences? Did someone get hurt, angry, frustrated, upset? Did it cause an argument or the dreaded silent treatment? Did that event cause the relationship to be fractured in some way?

I'm sure you're a good person. Yet, no matter how good you are, or even how good you *think* you are, there will have been times when you've stuffed up, right? Me too. We're all in this together. We all live in a world of mucky mud we've created from the consequences of our own actions. We are all stained by it. We haven't been able to come up with a solution on our own like a 'Wonder Powder Sin Stain Remover' that can take it all away. I wish there was! Wouldn't that make life so much easier? Wouldn't it be fabulous to walk through life without having to trudge?

The thing is, we've tried to come up with our own solutions to solving our mud issue. Some people solve it by simply denying it's a problem at all. They see life the way it is and accept that this is our muddied-up reality and don't look for a solution because they don't believe that a problem exists. Others try very hard to do good things, live a 'right' way and believe that if they just do enough good then that will, if not fix the problem, certainly help it. That's a better approach because better choices mean less mucky consequences, but it doesn't solve the mud problem.

Unfortunately, some of those who opt for this second approach often become stuck in a different textured mud. When we think we have the 'right' way of doing something we tend to try and impose our 'right' way on to other people who we see operating in the 'wrong' way. Can you see how this may create relational tension? Many conflicts arise because one person has their view on how something 'should' be done whilst the other person also thinks that *they* have the correct view on how things 'should' be done.

Where do all these 'shoulds' come from? We all have our unique upbringings, life experiences, belief and value systems, ideals, methods we've found useful for ourselves, things we've seen work in history… Our ideas of how things 'should' be done come from so many sources that it's hard to pinpoint their origins. What we do know is that if we feel that people 'should' be operating in 'our' way, that will inevitably lead us to want to control and change their behaviour.

As Christians, we hold on to what the Bible says very dearly. I love God's Word. I love studying the Bible, meditating on scripture, memorising passages, and allowing my life to be informed by the living, breathing Spirit of God. (2 Timothy 3:16-17, Hebrews 4:12) This is one of the essential tools we have by which we can align our hearts with God's and infuse our minds with the mind of Christ. (1 Corinthians 2:16)

The problem that we have faced as Christians throughout the centuries is in how we *interpret* scripture. I think it's important to note that **NONE of us have a fully correct interpretation of scripture.** It's impossible! Because our thoughts are shaped by knowledge and experiences which are tainted by mud. Despite how much we can potentially learn of God throughout our lives, we still only know 'in part'. (1 Corinthians 13:9) Our understanding of God is never complete, so – on this side of heaven – we will never have a perfect, *correct* viewpoint. This means that being humble and teachable are essential qualities to have when wading through murky theological issues. I must consider the possibility that I may need to adjust my thinking in line with new insights that may be more helpful, loving, and more in line with God's kingdom values and character. This includes being open and respectful to the ideas and life stories of others.

Appreciating this is imperative, because our interpretations of scripture form our understanding, which shape our beliefs. These beliefs have the potential to become our 'shoulds' when we turn them into rules which we impose on other people. At this point, the life-giving, Spirit-breathed scripture, which was designed to help people live vibrant, faith-filled, godly lives, becomes a weaponised, destructive tool to correct unwanted behaviour through fear, manipulation, and control. How that must break God's heart.

When the rules are applied, they become legalism. When legalism is enforced, the someone with the 'should' becomes the judge, jury, and executioner of that rule. They become a legal system unto themselves and will point the finger, declare that the person (or group) in question is in the 'wrong' and then deal out the consequences that they choose to impose. That could be as little as a 'tut-tut' naughty finger poke, to rejection from Christian community. Excommunication, it's called. "We no longer will communicate with you because you don't adhere to our rules. You are out of communion with us." That's harsh, but I've seen it happen. I have experienced it myself. So has my church.

It's quite possible that when Jesus was approached by those people asking him about fasting that they were coming to him with that finger-pointing approach. "Why are you telling your disciples they don't have to fast? That's not 'right'! That's not the way it is 'supposed' to be done, the way the Old Testament scriptures tell us to do it. That, after all, is the supreme authority in all spiritual matters. You're going against the rules! You're going against *God*."

Jesus doesn't take on board their attitudes. He doesn't answer their question the way they wanted or expected him to. He didn't try to defend or justify himself or use another law to counteract their legalistic expectations. He answered it by showing them a picture of who he is: a bridegroom. The disciples didn't need to fast because they were his guests, and guests don't need to fast if the bridegroom is with them. Full stop. Isn't that clear?

Probably not. I doubt that the disciples would have understood what Jesus meant when he shared with them that image. In fact, I believe that the whole reason why Jesus followed his bridegroom representation with an equally ambiguous note about wine and wineskins and patches of cloth was because they simply *wouldn't* get it. They couldn't. How could they have possibly understood? To understand, they had to re-think their thinking. They had to put this 'new wine' into new wineskins. They had to renew their minds.

What was it that the disciples were going to have to unlearn before they could embrace this new understanding that Jesus was presenting to them?

We are going to consider this in our next chapter as we take a dive into the pensieve of the Old Testament scriptures and look at the origins of the concept of marriage.

## Chapter 5
# THE BEGINNING OF UNIONS

Jesus' identification as a bridegroom would have connected with his audience's understanding of the meaning of marriage and weddings. They would have appreciated the concepts of commitment, communion, and celebration. They would have even recognised those same themes running through the scriptures.

The idea of God identifying himself as a bridegroom wasn't a new one. In the Old Testament, we read about God likening himself to a husband, betrothing himself to his people like a groom to his bride.

> **Isaiah 54:5-6:** "'For your Maker is your husband – the Lord Almighty is his name – the Holy One of Israel is your Redeemer; he is called the God of all the earth. The Lord will call you back as if you were a wife deserted and distressed in spirit – a wife who married young, only to be rejected,'" says your God."

> **Hosea 2:16, 19-20:** "'In that day,'" declares the Lord, "'you will call me 'my husband'; you will no longer call me 'my master'. I will betroth you to me forever; I will betroth you in righteousness and justice, in love and compassion. I will betroth you in faithfulness, and you will acknowledge the Lord.'"

Through these and other diverse accounts in scripture, people would have appreciated God's commitment to them. God's presence was represented in the institution of the original tabernacle and construction of temples of worship. It was manifested through powerful signs and wonders. God reassured his people of his faithfulness and offered guidance through the prophets. God demonstrated how much he valued communion with his people, walking with Adam and Eve in the garden, to being symbolised by the Ark of the Covenant. There could be no doubt that this God, Yahweh, was with them, was committed to them, and desired a special partnership with them. And of course, there was celebration. They knew how to mark milestones. They celebrated good times and lamented hard times, and they did it as a community.

Drawing on his audience's strongly founded understanding of these key concepts allowed Jesus to communicate profoundly to his listeners. He added layers of meaning to them as he taught. It was an *introduction* to a radical, far greater understanding that would take his entire ministry to encapsulate. Perhaps this can only be seen in hindsight, looking at the panoramic picture of Jesus' life and ministry. To do that, we need to start right back at the beginning...

Where did this idea of marriage and unions come from? Where did Jesus' audience's understanding begin?

If you can imagine a pensieve with me, we're going to take a verse out of Genesis and pop it in. It's the first verse in the Bible that describes a type of union between two people, which we have come to describe as a 'marriage'.

> **Gensis 2:24:** "That is why a man leaves his father and mother and is united to his wife, and they become one flesh."

Let's jump into that Bible verse. Picture yourself either reading this text or listening to it being it taught. Can you remember a time that may have been? It's ok if you can't. But unless you're reading it for the first time, you'll already have your own understanding of what it means, determined by your age, your religious denomination, and the viewpoints of those who taught you. Because of this, we will each have our own understanding of what this passage means.

I want to acknowledge that it can be hard to dive into a passage of scripture to try and understand it from a different perspective. We only know what we know, right? Most of us haven't grown up in the Jewish culture, so I recognise that this dip into our pensieve is limited without being able to take some historical Jewish thoughts with us to understand what they were thinking.

When I was growing up, this verse meant 'leaving and cleaving'. I was taught that when we got married, we had to leave our parents and cleave to our partner. That was the essence of marriage: forming a union with your spouse having left your family to create a new one. With this interpretation, Jesus would have been saying to his listeners something along the lines of, "I am so committed to you that I chose to *leave* my Father (parent figure) in heaven so that I can *cleave* to you, i.e. form an intimate relationship to create our own union."

Let's add another verse to our pensieves.

# THE BEGINNING OF UNIONS

**Genesis 1:28:** "God blessed them and said to them, '"Be fruitful and increase in number; fill the earth and subdue it.'" *(Abbreviated)*

> It seems that the point of a union was
> for the purpose of reproduction.
> It's right there. The first mandate God
> gave to people: "Go make babies."
> And, as a population, they were to 'subdue' the earth.

To me, the first part of the mandate makes sense. God had given Adam and Eve (the protagonist representatives of the human species in the Genesis creation story) a whole planet. It seems logical that God would want to fill it, so I'm not trying to be genderist or sexist in saying that it was God's mandate to populate the earth. The fact is there's a very practical, biological reality at work. We need both male and female 'bits' to make babies to populate the earth. Even Darwin would agree with that!

I have to say, I think we've done a pretty good job at procreation. With currently over eight billion people in the world do you think humanity has made a reasonable attempt to fill the earth? Sure, there are places that are geographically uninhabitable, but for the most part, we can see human influence across the globe. Just look at photos taken from space of the earth, particularly at night. You will see the lights of the world glimmering the shapes of our continents. It is a beautiful sight.

We'll delve into the idea of subduing the earth in greater detail later. For now, I'd simply like to introduce you to the idea of God giving humanity a mandate to be caretakers of this beautiful planet. Human beings were given the responsibility to look after it, cultivate it, and to help maintain it so that the world could flourish and all living beings could thrive on it, which help us survive and populate.

Combining these two verses of Genesis, we find God blessing the union of a man with his wife who were to populate the earth for the purpose of creating a world filled with flourishing communities that nurture the earth for the prosperity of all. It sounds wonderfully idyllic.

With this image in our pensieves, picture Jesus, declaring himself to be a bridegroom, and (albeit indirectly and cryptically) telling the people who were challenging him that he was God's representative on earth. His disciples didn't need to fast because he was God with them. Jesus was going to show his disciples a new, radical way of living by faith and provide them with instruction and his own personal example of what that looked like. He was going to teach them to put new wine into new wineskins (to re-think their thinking), so that they could believe and act upon a **new mandate,** which he would reveal to them at the very end – just before he would no longer be with them in person. What a way to start his ministry!

Spoiler alert: The new mandate is related to Jesus being the bridegroom but has *nothing* to do with populating the earth.

"WHAT?!?"

I'm going to let you ponder that for a moment.

For now, just know that there *is* a new mandate. There *is* a new way of thinking. There *is* a new purpose for the church, but it doesn't look like the old thinking. It's not the old mandate anymore. Jesus has a purpose for us, but it's different. To understand it, we are going to have to re-think what we think about marriage, about ministry, about many things we may think we know but may need to take a fresh look at. To receive the new, we first must become new vessels to put it in. As the apostle Paul so eloquently put it, we need to be 'transformed by the renewing of our minds.' (Romans 12:2)

I pray that by the end of reading this book you will be able to understand the new mandate, embrace it, re-think it, and believe it, so you can live it wholeheartedly. Doing this has the potential to change how we live out our faith and the impact we will have on our world.

Sounds exciting, doesn't it?

The problem that we must face before we get there is still the problem of the mud. We live in an imperfect world. There is so much brokenness in relationships, marriages, and even churches.

> **We live with unkept commitments, broken communion, and we struggle to celebrate together because of the dysfunction amongst us.**

To make things worse, whilst we're already in this state of muddiness, along come the finger-pointing wedding planners who think they have something that is *just right* to make everything perfect.

But does it?

# Chapter 6

# THE WEDDING PLANNER'S ATTITUDE

"Leave your father and mother. Be united with your wife. Become one flesh. Have children, populate, and 'subdue' (or rule / take care of / be a steward of) the earth." (Genesis 2:24 and Genesis 1:28, *Paraphrased*)

That's where we left off: the beginning of the idea of a union. I left us there on purpose to let those verses from Genesis simmer in our pensieves for a little bit. Where did our understanding of these verses come from? What, when, and who helped us understand our interpretation of these passages of scripture?

Why is this so significant? Because the interpretations of these scriptures – for better or for worse – have become embedded into Christian thinking and Christian culture. Not only that, but they have also been rigidly set in laws all over the world. In Australia, up until 2017, same sex marriages were not legally permitted. There are other cultures throughout history who have adopted even more extreme legislation of these scriptures, determining that any sex outside of 'sex that *leads directly to reproduction*' is not only sinful, but illegal. How did we get this way? How did those laws and societal rules get passed and accepted by so many for so long?

I believe that this application is well-intentioned, by people wanting to adhere as closely as possible to the ideals of the Bible, who have wanted to follow God's Word as best as they can, for their own good and for the wellbeing of their communities. In our metaphor, these people are our lovely, experienced, neatly dressed wedding planners.

Wedding planners see the issue. They see the mud. They see the sin of the world. Wedding planners also see a solution. They have a piece of pristine fabric they think will be the world's solution: like these two verses in Genesis. Are they beautiful verses? Yes. Are they idyllic for the formation of families, procreation of our species, and survival of humankind? Yes.

To build families with both a loving father and mother present, who unconditionally love one another and perfectly raise their children in a safe, protected home where they can be nurtured is idyllic. Wouldn't we all want that? Perfect parents. Perfect children. Perfect home. Everyone purposeful and flourishing. Everyone accepting, caring, and supporting one another, loving each other and loving God together. That was the original plan. It was a brilliant plan. It's a wonderful idea to aspire to. Under those conditions it makes perfect sense to say, "Go! Multiply! Fill the world with lots and lots of loving families that will make wholesome, thriving communities who will all work for the greater good and feel fulfilled in contributing to the wellbeing of society. Off you go!" What could possibly go wrong?

Let's go back to our story... We have a stunning bride. She's all ready for her wedding. When she was offered her engagement ring, everything was perfect. She was perfect. Their relationship was perfect. She expected everything to go perfectly as she approached the church.

When God created human beings, he created them in his marvellous image with the character of God and his goodness, along with instilling in them the values of heaven. He walked with them (in this case, with our symbolic representatives, Adam and Eve, in a garden) in a perfect union with one another. But something went wrong…

Splutter and ka-thunk.

Trust got broken. That's the moral of the story of 'the fall of humankind' found in the early chapters of Genesis. When trust got broken, sin (everything that is not of trust or faith in God) entered the world and all that was pristine became muddy. The bride stepped out of her perfect world and entered the mud. The promise of a relationship was there. She knew her partner wanted to spend the rest of his life with her. She also knew that to get to him she was going to have to walk through the mud. And she did.

We wade through sin. Every day. It gets in us and on us. It's all around us. We trudge through it. We stumble. We fall. We can't get rid of the mud problem for ourselves. It's easy to feel helplessly stuck and that life becomes a fight against it. All. The. Time.

When the bride arrived at the church with a torn dress, completely covered in muck, she was greeted by the wedding planner who thought she had THE solution. She pulled out a piece of pure, white fabric and pinned it on to her dress, truly believing that this would fix the tear and cover the mud. All she could see was the white piece of material…

That's what we do with this piece of scripture. I don't know if you've recognised this, but these words from Genesis were issued in the context of a perfect world. They were spoken in the context of a perfect relationship between God and man and one another. It was *before* that relationship got broken, before the muck of sin entered the world, and yet we try and apply these scriptures to *every* marriage and family in *every* cultural context throughout the history of the world and we wonder why it doesn't fit and why it doesn't work. It doesn't work because of the mud. Mud muddies EVERYTHING!

There are two problems with the legalistic wedding planner approach. The first is that, despite their good intentions, all they see is the white patch of material. Anything outside of that is criticised, judged, excluded, rejected, ostracised. And pins that are used to fasten the fabric on don't hold it in place. They tear the dress and make it worse. It's true. They make the situation worse.

The second problem is (and I don't want to burst anyone's idealistic bubble about relationships here) **there are no perfect relationships.** The white patch doesn't make the muddy dress clean. The opposite happens. The white patch becomes muddy.

Let me make it clear: it is wonderful to aspire to have idyllic relationships, especially when it comes to marriage. But it's not our place to judge, humiliate, or reject people who don't attain that, because none of us can.

In our metaphor, no matter how well-intentioned the wedding planner's motives were, the application of her strategy was an inappropriate response to the problem. It was an attempt to fix a problem with a 'one size fits all' approach that didn't work. In fact, it caused destruction rather than creating a solution.

This was true in my life, in my relationship with my husband. When I was nineteen, I looked for the godliest man I could find, and I married him. We ticked all the boxes. We did everything by 'The Book'. We did it right. And by all Christian standards it should have worked. But it didn't and by the end of 23 years of marriage it was muddied, torn, and broken.

When we separated, I had well-intentioned people try and tell me to go back, stick it out, fix what was broken. They took this white patch of fabric and tried to pin it on my broken marriage.

I was told things like:

- "You'll never fulfill God's purpose for your life if you leave this man."
- "You'll miss out on all the blessings of God if you get divorced."
- "The only way to live a God-honouring life is to stick it out."
- "If you leave, it's because you don't have enough faith in God to restore things."
- "If you divorce, you'll lose your salvation."

All these types of comments I was issued were like bullets to my heart. Rather than being offered gracious wisdom and care, Bible verses were weaponised and used against me. They heaped a burden of guilt on me that I could no longer fulfil my wifely duties and promises as I had hoped, as if I didn't feel guilty enough already.

No one wants their marriage to fail. We don't intentionally set out to sabotage it. It's more likely that little smudges of muddy, unaddressed sin gradually stain and tear at it until it's gone too far. Divorce was my tragic outcome. In the end, all I felt was blame, shame, and guilt.

Those wedding planners in my world fastened their interpretations of scripture onto my broken marriage. Despite their good intentions they made things worse, so much worse. I was already acutely aware of my own failings and what I had contributed to our marital breakdown. I am neither innocent, nor a victim. I was already covered in mud, but when people pointed their judgemental fingers at me, it made me feel criticised, judged, excluded, and ultimately rejected by them because I could no longer keep up the facade of a perfect marriage, nor return to a relationship that I felt was hurting me. I left feeling condemned and found myself displaced from my family and home that I had loved so deeply for so long, which I had tried so hard to build on faith and God's Word. I was covered in mud. My heart was shattered.

Fortunately, that wasn't the end of the story…

# Part 3
## THE BLANKET

# THE BRIDEGROOM'S WOVEN BLANKET
## *Scene 3*

The groom heard his bride sobbing. Now, we know that the groom isn't supposed to see the bride before the wedding, but he defied tradition and came out anyway. He picked her up and wiped her tears. He held her in his arms.

She tried to pull away.

The groom sensed her shame and embarrassment and held her reassuringly, lifting her head so she could look in his eyes.

"I love you," he said, "with all my heart. You are more beautiful to me now than you have ever been."

The bride couldn't believe what she was hearing. She didn't feel beautiful. All she felt was terrible shame.

"How can that possibly be?" she asked. "Look at me. I'm covered in mud."

She stepped back so he could see all the muck that covered her.

"My lovely bride," he replied, "when I look at you, I see absolute perfection. I don't see mud. I see your beautiful heart. A heart that devotedly loves me, that would wade through filth to reach me, to be with me – forever."

At that moment, the bride felt he could see right through her, to the core of her being. She felt naked and exposed yet completely loved. He was right. She loved him, more than anything else in the whole world.

The groom took her hands in his, looking at her sparkling engagement ring.

"It's going to be ok. I promise. I knew about the mud. I've got this sorted. I have a wonderful surprise for you: the most gorgeous, sparkling, clean dress is on its way. Trust me. You'll love it and look stunning."

The bride, for the first time, felt a glimmer of hope spread through her, but then she saw her stained dress…

It was like her husband could read her mind.

"Wait here," he said, as he disappeared into the church and brought out a big, white box, tied with a golden ribbon.

"You bought me a *gift*?" the bride asked incredulously, but her husband-to-be just smiled at the love of his life and gave her the box.

Gently and curiously, she took it and untied the ribbon. She lifted the lid and saw the most beautiful hand-woven blanket she had ever seen. She gasped.

"Did you… did you weave this yourself?" She knew he was a craftsman, but never suspected that he knew how to weave, and certainly not this expertly.

He smiled and nodded. "A man of hidden talents," he winked.

"I… I can't believe it. It's incredible."

As she took the blanket out of the box, she discovered intricate patterns and pictures that representing shared memories, blended with colours reflecting each season of the relationship they'd cultivated. There were bright golds and pinks and purples, and darker hues of greys and blues and greens. There were symbolic tear drops and rays of sunshine, images representing special moments that filled their universe. In the centre of it all was a tree. She recognised it instantly. It left her breathless…

"It's our tree," she whispered. "Where we met."

He nodded.

"You and I are amazing together. Think about how much we've been able to do and give already, and our life together has barely begun." He squeezed her hand and kissed her forehead.

"I don't know what to say. How can I thank you?" she asked sincerely.

"Well, put it on!" he exclaimed, wrapping it around her shoulders, covering her beautifully. Despite its rich texture it felt so soft and light, gracing her in a magnificent woven tapestry of story and colour.

The groom thought his heart would burst as she twirled around in the woven blanket.

"You don't need to see the mud anymore, sweetheart. Just look at *this* and remember the beautiful life we are weaving together."

Then he took her in his arms and whispered tenderly, "I am still committed to you. I love you unconditionally. Don't be ashamed or embarrassed. All *I* want is to marry you and celebrate our life together forever. Do you still want that with *me*?"

Wrapped in her glorious, woven blanket, with glistening tears and a beaming smile, the bride held her future husband's hand and spoke words that flowed from the depths of her heart.

"I do."

## Chapter 7

# BLANKETS OF LOVE – HANDWOVEN BY JESUS

Jesus, the bridegroom, offered his beautiful bride a hand-woven blanket to cover her. It didn't take away the mud, or the effects and consequences of the mud, but it completely covered her, allowing her to live in a world of muck and not have to focus on it, but on the one who wove the blanket for her.

The threads used to weave this blanket are all the beautiful designs we find Jesus weaving throughout the gospels, that he demonstrated in practical ways throughout his life. I'd encourage you to go back through the New Testament books of Matthew, Mark, Luke, and John and look at Jesus, simply focusing on his interactions with others and see how graciously and beautifully he loved.

Jesus offers each one of us the same gift of love. In our metaphor, this love is represented by a personally hand-woven blanket, uniquely tailored to suit us as individuals, decorated with symbols, patterns, and colours that reflect the stories of our life with him. Our blankets are a depiction of a life of faith that we weave with him, which is expressed in love.

Our lives have different themes for different seasons, many of which are universally relatable as human beings. Some of those patterns we've looked at are commitment, communion, and celebration. These relate to the idea of Jesus being a bridegroom and the association with weddings.

In Chapter 2 we looked at the ways Jesus taught his followers to re-think the kingdom of God throughout his ministry. Whilst he taught with many different methods about lots of different things, what do you think was his most common theme?

Love. That's right! Absolutely. Jesus taught his followers how to love. In fact, he took the Old Testament law and summarised it with one simple, overarching instruction:

> **Mark 12:30-31:** "Love the Lord your God with all your heart and with all your soul and with all your mind and with all your strength… *(and)* love your neighbour as yourself. There is no commandment greater than these." *(Abbreviated)*

This summary is also found in Matthew 22:37-40 and Luke 10:27. Rather than trying to teach his disciples how to apply the myriads of Old Testament laws, Jesus umbrellaed them in one all-encompassing principle and then taught his followers how to weave love into everything they did. In doing this, Jesus showed them how to turn the blanket into a poncho! He taught them to *put on love,* so to speak.

> **Colossians 3:12-14:** "Therefore, as God's chosen people, holy and dearly loved, clothe yourselves with compassion, kindness, humility, gentleness, and patience. Bear with

each other and forgive one another if any of you have a grievance against someone. Forgive as the Lord forgave you. And over all these virtues put on love, which **weaves** them all together in perfect unity." *(Bold and paraphrase mine.)*

The poncho acts like a covering for the mud. When Jesus taught people to love one another he was weaving the universal summary of Old Testament law through everything he said. His teaching was, in essence, along these lines: "In everything that you do, every decision that you make, everything that you say – think about how you're *being love*."

Jesus embodied this in the way he interacted with people. Instead of rigidly following Old Testament law, he taught his disciples how to apply the law of love. He ate with sinners, touched people with leprosy, spoke with rejected women, and healed sick people on the sacred Sabbath day, which was supposed to be a day of rest. He modelled through his actions that relationships mattered more than rules. His unconventional approach caused dissension and unrest amongst the legalistic religious leaders of the time, yet Jesus refused to give in to their rigid expectations, showing the people (and us) how to think beyond those laws to a higher ethic through love. Love covers it all.

Let's go now to the end of Jesus' ministry. It was the last night before he was to die, and we find him sitting with his disciples around the table, the bridegroom with his guests.

Just as we correlated the weaving of commitment, communion, and celebration to a wedding, we can also do the same with the sacramental act of communion. A sacrament is something that we do that symbolises something else. For example, being immersed in the waters of baptism represents dying to our old life and rising from the water to a new life with

Jesus. That's a sacramental act. We also take communion. We drink wine or juice and eat some form of bread in a symbolic representation of Jesus' last supper. It is sacramental because of what Jesus used it to represent that night.

In sharing this meal with his disciples, Jesus was assuring them one last time of his unwavering commitment to them. He was saying, "I am committed to fulfilling God's plan of salvation for you – 'till my final breath."

This was a huge deal. Jesus knew what was coming. Events had already been set in motion that would take him to the cross. As the plan unfolded, his mind was focused and his purpose would not be thwarted, despite the agonising pain he knew he would go through on our behalf. It's no wonder when Jesus prayed later in the evening that sweat-like drops of blood would seep through his skin. (Luke 22:44) This was an extraordinary commitment. In this, Jesus was telling his disciples, "I will give my life for you so you can be with me forever." He knew the suffering he would go through would secure our union with him. There was no doubt in his mind. There was no going back. His resolve was sure.

This special meal Jesus celebrated with his disciples was at the time of the Passover feast. It commemorated the sparing of Hebrew households from death, consequently liberating the Jewish people from Egypt in what is known as the Exodus. The angel of death would 'pass over' their homes when it saw lamb's blood smeared on their door frames. (Exodus 12) The Exodus marked the beginning of a ritual practiced in Jewish tradition of the sacrifice of unblemished lambs (lambs without any defects). The blood of the lambs represented purity and innocence and was sprinkled on the altar at the temple as an offering of atonement for the sin of the people who brought it. This marked a profound image of reconciliation with God.

Now, Jesus would bring his own meaning to the Passover.

Jesus took the bread and the cup and offered them to his disciples explaining that this was his body, which would be broken for them, and his blood that would be shed for them. He asked them to keep this ritual as a way of remembering what he was about to do on their behalf. (Matthew 26:26-30, Luke 22:13-20) In doing this, Jesus was no longer referring to the historical events of the Jews. Instead, he was indicating the miraculous liberation from sin that he would achieve for them (and us) by his demonstration of love on the cross the following day. The disciples didn't know it at the time. How could they?

How could they possibly comprehend that the man sitting with them sharing their meal would choose to become that very same symbolic representation on behalf of humanity? Jesus' death would be the fulfilment of the Old Testament prophecy in Isaiah 53:7b who would be led to the cross like a lamb to the slaughter.

Jesus, like the spotless lamb, was the only one who has walked this earth through the mud and not been smeared and dirtied by it. That was what made him the only one who was qualified to sacrificially die on our behalf. (2 Corinthians 5:21) One offering – by one man – for all humankind. (Romans 5:17-19) Thank you, Jesus!

To ensure we would be with him forever, Jesus had to solve the 'splutter-ka-thunk' issue: the broken trust that allowed sin into the world. In other words, the problem of the mud. Jesus knew that by offering himself to die it would represent to God that he was taking upon himself the mess that humanity has made. Through his death, he would take care of our sin and mess once and for all. (Hebrews 10:10-14)

In becoming like that spotless lamb, Jesus' innocent blood became a representation of atonement and the means of reconciliation with God for all people. (Hebrews 10:1-18) After his death, ritual sacrifices were no longer required because when we believe in Jesus, his symbolic act 'protects' us in the same way the blood of the lamb being smeared on the doorframes protected the Hebrew households. When we believe in Jesus, our faith acts as a protective covering and God no longer sees the sin that causes our relationship with him to be broken. Jesus' love acts like a huge, woven blanket, concealing it all. Our sins are forgiven. There is no longer a division between us and him because, in God's eyes, the broken trust has been dealt with through Jesus. Jesus' death was the ultimate sacramental act.

This, however, doesn't mean that the consequences of sin are dealt with. We still live in a world of mucky mud. We find ourselves salvaging the fallout of our decision-making. We make mistakes. We slog it out. We stumble. We trudge.

The good news is that Jesus offers us two important things to hope for:

1. In the mucky mud Jesus has promised to be with us (Matthew 28:20b) - no matter what. Not only that, he invites us into a loving partnership with him where we can know him intimately and discover how to weave a life of faith expressing itself in love.
2. Jesus also gives us an eternal hope. This mucky state won't last. It's not the end – not by a long shot. We were created as eternal beings for an eternal life. When Jesus rose from the dead, he showed us that a resurrected life is possible and that the endgame is an eternity with him in a perfected world. As in our metaphor, brand new, pristine clothes for everyone! (1 Corinthians 15)

The Last Supper would be a reminder to the disciples (and to all of us) that Jesus chose to become the image of the spotless lamb who would demonstrate love through his own life offering. That perfect offering provided a means for the muddy sin problem to be solved. For now, in part... But in the future, for good. Done away. Dealt with. Kaput.

## Chapter 8

# OUR UNIQUELY PERSONALISED BLANKETS

Jesus was the embodiment of love. He radically and unwaveringly demonstrated this throughout his time on earth. There was something uniquely attractive about him that inspired people to follow him. What was that *something*?

His love gracefully allowed people to flourish.

Finding a place where we can flourish within a community can often be a challenge. There are so many ways in which we criticise, discriminate, judge, and exclude one another. In contrast, Jesus was warm and inviting. He welcomed people with open arms, even the outcasts of society, and made them feel valued and special, because to him they genuinely were.

Jesus succinctly told us that the best thing we could possibly do in our human existence is to love God with our whole being, and to love one another *as* we love ourselves. It perfectly encapsulates the highest value of who God is, and our purpose for being.

> **The 'law of love' is like a three-fold weaving of God, us and others.**

The first instruction is to "love God with all our hearts, minds, souls, and with all our strength." This is an invitation into a loving partnership that comes from cultivating our relationship with him. The second part instructs us to love our neighbours. We'll explore these in more detail in later chapters. For now, I'd like to focus on the last part: *as* you love yourself.

There are four ways we could look at this little conjunction *'as'*.

1. As = Whilst. Jesus could have been telling his followers to love their neighbours *whilst* (at the same time as) they practiced loving themselves.
2. As = To the same degree. Jesus may have been referring to the amount of time and energy to invest in ourselves so that we are equipped to love others.
3. As = In the same manner. Jesus could have been referring to the reference of 'do to others as you would have them do to you' (treat others as you'd like to be treated) principle. (Matthew 7:12)
4. As = Being your genuine self. Jesus could have been inviting people to simply 'be themselves', authentically giving of themselves in loving others.

I'd like to suggest that the application of this principle of love is a combination of all four.

"Come as you are," Jesus invites.

"Who, *me*?"

"Yes, YOU!"

Jesus' love extends to all of us, freely, graciously, and unconditionally.

- No matter what race, culture, or language spoken…
- No matter our age, height, weight, state of health, or level of physical ability…
- No matter our sexual identity, gender, or sexual preferences…
- No matter our level of intelligence, educational experience, economic status, or position in society…
- No matter our beliefs, values, religious background, or life experiences…
- No matter our mistakes, failures, or even outright harmful things we've done…

Jesus welcomes us to his family. There is no exclusion policy, no fine print at the bottom of the contract, no requirement on our behalf. It's simply an open invitation to come. (Luke 14:15-23) There is nothing we need to change. There is nothing we need to do. We are infinitely and deeply loved – just as we are. We are already approved, valued, known, and treasured. If we choose to love him, it's because he loved us first. (1 John 4:19)

One of the exceptional aspects of Jesus' love is his acceptance of people. He invites them into a relationship with him in which he encourages individuals to get to know him intimately, like a courtship. It's an invitation to share life in all its highs and mucky lows, all the laughter and salty tears, all the heartache and the fruitful successes – together.

We have the privilege of doing this with him - just as we are. There is no imposition to change, no time frame set, no requirements to be fulfilled. It is a relationship where we can rest and simply 'be'. We can be angry with him. We can vent our loneliness when he feels distant. We can be frustrated, cranky, and confused. That's ok. We can also marvel in wonder at who he is and the world he's made. We can be grateful for the life we have and the people we share it with. We can learn and grow in the context of our relationship with Jesus, and we can have our hearts filled with his love.

It is in this intimate and vulnerable, yet safe and protected, relationship that we can find a place of true authenticity. This is the beginning place, and the one in which we are intended to remain in, before we give of ourselves in service to others, and *whilst* we're continuing to serve. This is the most important aspect of Christian living because it is out of this place of authentic, restful intimacy that everything else flows. This is where we find healing for our hearts, especially when they've been wounded in service to others. This is where we commune with Jesus and align our hearts and minds with his so that we can carry out projects and plans in our families and communities. This is where we celebrate and commemorate the ups and downs of the roller coaster of life. This is also where we find courage to stay committed to living out the values of his kingdom because the reality is: living in a muddy world is hard. So hard. At times, harder than we ever imagined, especially when we choose to live according to God's values and reflect his character. It can feel like we're wading counter-culturally against a strong current of social norms and expectations. It can be exhausting! Yet Jesus promises to be with us through it.

It's so important to invest time in cultivating our relationship with Jesus, making time to Stop. Revive. Survive. Burnout from serving others is an all-too-common problem amongst Christians who give and give without knowing how to balance life and stay connected with Jesus whilst they are giving. I know this all too well from personal experience. Jesus never asks us to be a martyr, nor a doormat, nor a punching bag for people to abuse. If you have found yourself in a place where you've been hurt because you've given too much, or where people have treated you badly, there is hope. Jesus came to restore the broken-hearted. (Psalm 147:3) To find that restorative healing, we must stay connected with Jesus.

Jesus used a helpful example of a vine to illustrate this.

> **John 15:5:** "I am the vine; you are the branches. If you remain in me and I in you, you will bear much fruit; apart from me you can do nothing."

Remaining in Jesus (abiding) is a significant part of self-love because it helps stop us from having to strive and struggle, trying to love others in our own strength. Why? Because we don't have to generate love towards others, we can simply rest in Jesus and allow ourselves to be conduits of his love. HE does all the work *through* us.

This is why it is vital to guard our hearts. (Proverbs 4:23) Everything we do and the words we say flow from it. (Matthew 12:34b) For this, learning to establish personal boundaries is essential. Carving out time to refresh our hearts, listen to God, learn from him, and maintain our relationship with him is a vital part of self-love.

As one who developed strong people-pleasing habits growing up, I'm learning to use the word 'no.' I am practising being more assertive in maintaining personal boundaries. I am still working on finding a healthy work/life balance; between giving to others whilst still caring for myself.

Can I invite you to consider how you are caring for your own heart? Are there things you could do to help you nourish your soul and cultivate your relationship with Jesus? He wants you to not just survive through life, but to flourish in it. If you don't feel like you're flourishing, what is it that you need? Who could you ask to help?

The personalised, woven blanket that Jesus offers is like a cosy, warm protection for your heart. Your heart is your most precious possession. It is of infinite worth. It is the centre of your distinctive 'you-ness'.

What are some things that are distinctively 'you'? What are aspects of your personality that you love about yourself? Discovering and holding on

## OUR UNIQUELY PERSONALISED BLANKETS

to our self-worth is vital to be able to give to others with both authenticity and clear boundaries. This has to do with how we view ourselves.

Our identities are our strongly formed perceptions of who we are, which were shaped by the experiences we've had, especially in our childhood. The way we were treated, the things significant people said to us and about us, and the way those experiences made us feel are reflected in how we see ourselves. In other words, our self-identity is largely based on how we perceive the way others view us. Once that perspective is established, it's very hard to change. If our sense of self is negative and unhelpful, we can do things like work on our mindset and self-talk. We can seek help from a coach, counsellor, or psychologist. And we can also ask Jesus what *he* thinks.

Because so much of our self-identity is based on external life experiences, having a loving voice that speaks into our hearts can change our life narrative. God uniquely and magnificently created us. There is no other you but YOU! You are unquestionably loved, purposefully designed, and intimately known. When we allow him to speak to us and share *his* heart for us, our identities become a truer representation of who we really are, because they are being formed by the original designer. Knowing who we are in relationship with Jesus gives us the clearest, most detailed, yet panoramic perspective because he chose us before the creation of the world and knows our significance to him for all the ages to come, along with all the minute details of every aspect of our lives. (Ephesians 1:4, 1 Corinthians 8:3)

Jesus invites us to be ourselves with him so that we can learn to value ourselves for who we **are,** not who we *used to* be or who we wished we *could* be. He helps us find self-acceptance for our wonderful attributes, as well as the harder things to love, like our flaws and failures. He wants us to practise appreciating our individual distinctiveness, which includes our quirky personalities, weird bents, and crazy ideas. This is how our personalised, woven blankets all end up so brilliantly unique. As human beings wonderfully designed and created by God (Psalm 139:13-16), learning to love who we genuinely are is one of the most precious things we can do in our lifetime. When we appreciate who we are, we can then begin to offer ourselves in distinctively marvellous ways to others.

**When we learn to love ourselves as
God loves us, we flourish.**

## Chapter 9

# DEALING WITH OUR OWN MUDDY MESS

"Secure your own oxygen mask first, before attempting to assist other passengers."

That's what we hear the flight attendants say as they model the pre-flight safety procedures. We know it makes sense. We can't help others if we can't take care of ourselves.

So many times, like our bride at the footsteps of the church, we find ourselves in a muddied state hoping for someone to come along and love us just as we are. That is what the bridegroom does. No matter where we find ourselves in life, Jesus comes to us in whatever state we're in and offers us his handwoven blanket of love. He lifts our heads, restores our dignity, and embraces us warmly. He helps us sort out our muddy issues so that we can have the capacity to look after ourselves before we try and look after others. It is from that restful place of connection that we can simply breathe, before we go about handing out oxygen masks to others.

In our story, the bride didn't dare enter the church to find her husband-to-be because she was too ashamed of the state she was in. Guilt and shame are two things that make us feel disconnected from God and others, and keep us feeling like we don't belong, because we feel that if people knew who we *really* are, and the messes we've made, we would never be accepted and loved. Maybe that's you? Perhaps you've already experienced the hurt of rejection because of your mistakes. I empathise with your pain.

We humans can make BIG messes! And people discredit us because of the things we've done. We can be shunned, blamed, laughed at, humiliated, disregarded, disrespected, unloved… Our actions do have consequences, and when we hurt other people, it inevitably breaks our relationships. That's the nature of living in the mud.

Let's slosh in and take a closer look at that murky mess.

'Sin' is an abstract term. It is like the words 'good' and 'evil'. They aren't tangible, meaning we can't see or touch them. Rather, they are used to create a common language to describe something. Sin is usually explained as the behaviour of someone that is wrong, bad, or against the rules. The Bible describes it as 'anything that does not come from faith'. (Romans 14:23b) I've referred to it previously, but what does it mean?

Let's take something scientific. Darkness is the absence of light. Darkness ceases to be dark in the presence of light. In the same way, sin is the absence of God's character and values. Whenever the character of God and the values of his kingdom are present, there is no sin. Instead, there is love. Where there is love, people flourish. God's love is woven into the fabric of our lives and finds expression in so many creative ways. It brightens our world.

There are lots of references to God and Jesus being light and bringing light, inviting us to be the light, and live in the light. (Some of these include John 1:5, 8:12, 12:36, Ephesians 5:8, 1 John 1:7, Matthew 5:14, 2 Corinthians 4:6.)

Where we see people acting with kindness, honesty, respect, courtesy, generosity, patience, or other noble qualities, we see God's kingdom values at work. We perceive them as being good because they promote the betterment of others. When we see people being abusive, disrespectful, aggressive, condescending, dishonest, self-promoting, proud, envious, greedy, and such, we recognise these as bad, wrong or, in cases of deliberate infliction of harm, evil. These things are destructive to others and break down society.

The nature of the kingdom of God is to promote the wellbeing of individuals, communities, and even the earth. When we align our thoughts and actions with this, we are living by faith. Christian faith is simply trusting that God's ways will promote our personal wellbeing and the wellbeing of our world, and hence we choose to live according to them.

**In other words, when we trust in the application of God's law of love in the way we live, we are living by faith in him.**

Faith means to trust. Christian faith is simply trusting in God, who revealed himself spectacularly in Jesus Christ, as love personified.

To trust God, we must first believe he exists; that there is a higher power at work in the universe. (Hebrews 11:6) This is the start of our faith journey that lasts for the rest of our lives, unless we irrevocably decide that there is absolutely no way that a higher power exists. What then unfolds is the exercising of that tiny faith muscle as we explore, learn, understand, and experience it.

Our exploration will inform how we view God, and this perspective will impact how we respond to God. If we believe God to be a harsh, punishing, vengeful, pain-inflicting God, we may hate or reject him. However, if we have a more positive experience, we may discover that God is love. If God is love, then his intentions towards us will be good and we can begin to believe that, despite how our circumstances may be, he still wants us to flourish as human beings.

When we appreciate aspects of the goodness of God, we begin to see the world through the lens of that goodness. Our vision changes and so do our beliefs and values. We begin to be shaped by the character of God and want to see more of his qualities expressed through our lives and live according to his kingdom values. We begin to live by faith, making decisions based on that belief foundation. At some point along the journey, we'll be able to look back and say, "Hang on! I'm not the same person that I used to be. I've changed. It's like I'm a new person."

> **2 Corinthians 5:17:** "Therefore, if anyone is in Christ, the new creation has come. The old has gone, the new is here!"

This radical, ongoing transformation happens uniquely, through our partnership with the Holy Spirit as we allow him to work in us. (2 Corinthians 3:18) It happens by ways and in timing that are *just right* for each of us. For some, it can happen so quickly that people may be astounded by the difference their faith has made, or it may take place so slowly that they barely perceive it happening.

Why is this important? Because this new creation can see themself and the world in a different way. One of our greatest limitations as human beings can be our inability to think or even imagine beyond what we currently know, understand, and experience. "This is how it's always been," we say. The way we've grown up, the things we were taught, and our life experiences shape how we see the world. It's hard to view beyond our defined perceptions, but the transforming work of the Holy Spirit makes this possible.

Our bride, crying on the steps of the church in her muddy dress, couldn't see past her dirty clothes. She couldn't see through her shame that she could possibly be accepted and loved as she was, let alone a future with her husband. Yet he came to her and showed her love. That's what Jesus does. He sees the state we're in and approaches us. In his presence, shame disappears because we are unconditionally loved. Just as the darkness cannot exist in the light, our shame cannot exist in the presence of God's love. Nor can fear. We don't have to fear punishment from God because love 'drives out fear'. (1 John 4:18)

I was like that bride. I described at the end of Part 2 how I was feeling shame and guilt related to my separation from my husband, and how that was made worse by those metaphorical wedding planners who pointed their fingers in judgement at me. When I look back at that season now, I liken it to spending decades setting a beautiful table for my whole extended family and closest friends, with elegant crockery and a stunning floral arrangement. I nourished everyone with food I provided. I helped them feel welcome and appreciated. Mealtime had the appearance of one big, happy family.

Except, the chair I was seated on was like a three-legged stool (like our law of love based on love of God, others, and ourselves). One of those legs over time got weaker and worn out, brittle, and fragile… I bet you can guess which one it was. I was ardently passionate about Jesus. I gave and gave with all the love I could give to my family, but I forgot to love myself in the process. I didn't voice how I was feeling burnt out, hurt, and lonely. I didn't address the issues in my marriage and the divide between us grew until we were no longer connected. I wanted to keep the peace, so I didn't make known my frustrations and struggles. I took it as self-sacrifice, becoming a martyr for the sake of being a good Christian, which I genuinely wanted to be. To say anything contrary would have been perceived as complaining which good Christians don't do.

Over time, I felt the stool becoming more and more unstable, until in one unexpected moment, it completely collapsed under me. I fell. I scrambled to hold tightly to the tablecloth. It slid with me, and everything that had been perfectly arranged on the table uncontrollably crashed into disarray. The unprecedented breakdown left my family and friends hurting. It created an empty space at the table where I had been, leaving my family to experience its aching emptiness. And me? I found myself seriously wounded in a crumpled heap. I was displaced from my family and home, separated from all that I had loved and cared about for decades. I lost everything I'd invested in. I went back to living with my parents, who graciously took me in. I struggled physically, financially, and emotionally, trying to reconfigure my life and heart, which would never be the same again.

That is the nature of the messiness of sin.

I never meant for all that to happen. I didn't plan it. Whilst I chose to leave my marriage, it was out of a sense of self-preservation and desperate brokenness, not because I wanted to. I never wanted to hurt my husband, children, or extended family. Yet I did. Badly. And I'm so, so sorry.

But, where we find more sin, we find even more grace. (Romans 5:20) That is the beauty of Jesus' woven blanket. I have experienced first-hand his grace and acceptance. When I felt lost and rejected, he covered my shame and loved me in my heartbreak.

The good news about Christianity is:

**Even if everyone around us rejects us and shames us for who we are or what we've done, we can find a place of acceptance and love in a relationship with Jesus.**

Jesus completely understands my heart. He knows all the million tiny events that led to that personal breakdown, beginning from my childhood and my desperate need for approval and recognition. He knows the baggage I brought into my marriage and how that unhelpfully worked itself out as the years unfolded. He also knows my husband's issues and how, together, our muddy mix contributed to our disconnection. Yet Jesus loved us both unconditionally through that mucky season. And still does.

I had to practise trusting Jesus in my brokenness, and trust him to care for my family, even when I couldn't be there. I had to trust him to heal my heart and restore my relationships where they had broken. My life now looks nothing like I'd ever imagined, but I still see God's hand of grace in it as I've picked up the pieces and started to rebuild, imagining new possibilities… Over this past decade, Jesus has renewed my heart and my faith, and I can look back over that season and gratefully say, "I am a new creation."

No matter what situation we're in or what we've done, Jesus doesn't condemn us, berate us, or belittle us. (Romans 8:1, Hebrews 4:16) He simply loves us. And whilst we're gently being held in that space of inclusion and grace, he kindly invites us to repent. (Romans 2:4)

Yes, we're back there again, re-thinking about thinking. Jesus asks us to think over what has happened, the things we've done (or failed to do) and consider how those actions, or inactions, have been detrimental to ourselves, our families, friends, communities, or the world. (2 Corinthians 7:11) When we're saddened by what we've done, Jesus doesn't make us feel guilty. Instead, he encourages us to start fresh, adjusting our behaviour in line with our new thinking, more aligned with his. (1 Corinthians 2:16b) In this way, we re-pent, re-think, re-align, and change the way we live, not only changing ourselves internally, but also in being agents of change for good in our world.

That is what God has done in me. My faith has been reconstructed and, whilst I still genuinely want to be a good person, I no longer see myself as a 'martyr for the cause', nor operate out of what I call 'spiritual duress' (doing Christian things because I *have* to, whilst feeling like an invisible, spiritual gun is being pointed at my head, like a threatening, '*or else!*') I am learning to have difficult, yet constructive, conversations to express how I genuinely feel, rather than bottling everything up inside. How I'm choosing to live is happier, healthier, more productive, and far more authentic.

**I'm free to look to the future and work out with Jesus how to care for others whilst still being self-sustaining.**

**So are you.**

If you've found yourself like the bride in our story, covered in muck, feeling ashamed or guilty for the things you've done, trust that Jesus' woven blanket of love is there to cover you. He knows your heart and wants to help you live a wholesome, abundant life. He wants you to experience the freedom that comes with living the law of love. He wants to heal your heart, work through the consequences of your decisions, and lead you in a new direction, with a fresh vision. That is the beauty of repentance.

Dealing with our own muddy issues with God is important so that we get our hearts in the right place and can then love others from a place of personal wellness and self-acceptance, *as* we love ourselves. However, if we waited until we were completely healed and have it all together, we'd be waiting our whole lives to start giving. We don't have to have *all* our issues sorted. We simply need to love with the capacity that we have, trusting that it is enough for today. That takes faith.

We don't know what tomorrow may bring. Tomorrow, we may have even greater capacity to give, or tomorrow our world may come unexpectedly crashing down around us and we may need more healing and restoration. We don't know. That's why God's grace is sufficient for us right now, in THIS moment. And that is enough. (2 Corinthians 12:9) If we need more, we can trust that he will provide it. (Philippians 4:19) If we lack it, there is no demand or expectation for us to offer more than we can.

## DEALING WITH OUR OWN MUDDY MESS

Having said that, sometimes God takes us out of our comfort zones, stretches our capacity, and helps us build our muscles of faith through the challenges we face. Through our hardships we develop character, perseverance, and resilience. (James 1:2-4, Romans 5:3-5) Like the muscles in our bodies, we can only build our faith muscle if we exercise it. We can trust that God will give us the strength and resources we need to get through whatever we're facing in his perfect timing.

When we live by faith, trusting in God's ways, we creatively find ways of expressing love in our everyday lives. As we practise self-care in the context of our relationship with Jesus, we will not only cultivate wellness within ourselves but will be stronger to support those around us. When we take care of ourselves, even though we may feel weak, hurt, or unwell, we can still come alongside other people and navigate this journey through the mud side by side.

We can do it TOGETHER.

# Part 4
## THE THREADS OF LOVE

# THE BRIDEGROOM'S WOVEN BLANKET

*Scene 4*

The bride stood with her future husband at the top of the stairs at the entrance of the church. They held one another tightly, reassuring each other of their beautiful promise of life together. The bride was covered in her woven blanket. The groom didn't see the mud, only her blanket adorned with the colours, symbols, and patterns of the life they were weaving together…

So enraptured were they in that moment, that the bride had failed to notice something significant: the absence of their guests. No one else had arrived. Where were they all?

A piercing cry in the distance popped their bubble of intimacy, as if to answer that very question. Not too far off, they could see someone approaching the church through the mud. They recognised one of their guests, injured by a fall, struggling to walk, covered in mud, worn-out, hurt, and helpless.

"We need to help him," the bride said to her groom with a worried look. She instinctively turned to race towards the guest. Unexpectedly, the groom took her hand, stopping her, pulling her in the opposite direction. He motioned toward an ornate, wooden door at the side of the church. With a puzzled look, the bride followed his lead.

The groom wasted no time. He hastened his steps. He opened the door, inviting her in. She entered and was overawed by what she saw: shelves filled with rows of boxes, hundreds, maybe thousands of personalised, hand-woven gifts for each guest, all named, but needing distribution.

"Will you help?" asked the groom.

"Nothing would give me greater pleasure. They'll *all* need a blanket," she replied, beginning to feel overwhelmed by the immensity of the project.

Again, the groom read her mind. "Just start with one," he instructed, handing her the box belonging to the injured man.

The bride took the box, stepped into the mud, and began wading towards the guest, who was now struggling to remain upright.

As she walked through the mud, she discovered something incredible: her blanket was made from a material that was non-stick! As mud couldn't stick, no matter how deep she had to wade, the blanket remained clean.

When she reached the gentleman, she embraced him wholeheartedly and offered him his gift. He opened it in wonder and put his blanket on. Being offered something so precious and so personal made him teary.

"My friend," said the bride. "It's going to be ok."

He looked at his blanket wrapped around him. It was so bright and beautiful that it radiated like sunshine in stark contrast to the mud. He wiped his eyes and looked back at the path he had trodden, which had felt like a *very… long…* way. As he gazed back, he saw other people approaching of all ages, sizes, genders, and cultures - all guests - all wading through the mud.

The bride and the guest instinctively knew what needed to be done. At precisely the same time they said, "Let's help them!"

## Chapter 10
# REPRESENTATIONS OF LOVE

There are lots of different ways in which we represent things. We use codes, symbols, maps, flags, logos, mascots, statues... A flag isn't a country, but it uses colours and symbols to *represent* a country, characterising how the nation wants to be perceived by the world.

When God chose to represent himself, he chose Jesus.

**Hebrews 1:3:** "The Son is the radiance of God's glory and the exact representation of his being." *(Abbreviated)*

This means that all the values of the kingdom and the character of God were represented perfectly in Jesus.

When Jesus came to earth, he was fully representing God, and yet he chose a range of ways to represent himself. To demonstrate who he was he used different imagery, saying things like, "I am the gate, the vine, the good shepherd, the light of the world, the bread of life, the way, the truth, and the life…" (John 10:7, 15:5, 10:11, 8:12, 6:35, 14:6) Out of the many images that Jesus used to describe himself, the one that is the focus of this book is Jesus as the bridegroom.

One of the most well-known texts regarding Jesus being the bridegroom for his bride, the church, is found in Revelation 21.

> **Revelation 21:2-5:** "I saw the Holy City, the new Jerusalem, coming down out of heaven from God, prepared as a bride beautifully dressed for her husband. And I heard a loud voice from the throne saying, '"Look! God's dwelling place is now among the people, and he will dwell with them. They will be his people, and God himself will be with them and be their God. He will wipe every tear from their eyes. There will be no more death or mourning or crying or pain, for the old order of things has passed away.'"

This is such a fantastic verse, full of hope and vision for a perfected future with God. It's a glimpse of heaven represented by two different pictures: on one hand, an image of a bride and, on the other, a city. John, the author of Revelation, is combining these illustrations to form an even greater image.

When I picture a city, I think of multitudes of people, like the city of Sydney, Tokyo, Delhi, Mexico City, or New York – masses and masses of people – millions of humans living in the one area. When I think of a bride, beautifully dressed, all ready for her wedding, I get the feeling that she's an excited lover waiting to start her new life committed to her husband. Putting those images together, we have:

1. A massive, whopping number of people congregated.
2. All wanting to commit to God and live with him forever.

What a picture!

## REPRESENTATIONS OF LOVE

In this combined image we can see once again the patterns we've been weaving. We can see commitment. This verse describes a 'forever'. We are eternal, spiritual beings living in earthly, fragile bodies. As the spiritual, eternal part of us lives on, we believe by faith that our life with God and one another isn't just for our time on earth, but forever. We can also see communion as God's dwelling place is, and will forever be, with his people. Celebration also weaves its way into this passage because there will be no more death or pain. What an awesome way to celebrate eternity! But as we've also said in previous chapters, none of that could have happened without Jesus' demonstration of love on the cross.

Remember when we talked about the original concept of a union and the mandate given to populate and take care of the earth? (Genesis 2:24 and Genesis 1:28) Well... now we're going to bring these ideas together. This is where it gets cool!

I don't believe the verses in Genesis about a 'union between a man and a woman' were written as a formula for every single relationship, in every culture throughout history. I also don't think they were intended as rules or laws that we should impose on people, especially if we add criticism or judgement (like our metaphorical wedding planners) when they don't meet this ideal. Our muddy reality is that none of our relationships meet a perfect ideal, so why do we judge one another when we don't live up to a perfect standard?

What I do believe, however, (and this is the beauty of representations and symbols) is that this image from Genesis is one of the first prophetic pictures we have of Jesus:

> **Jesus was going to leave his parent-figure in heaven to come to earth to become one *of* us, so he could become united *with* us for eternity.**

**The purpose?**
**To create a *family of faith* throughout history.**

What an amazing plan!

And that's not all!

Let's go back to the original mandate: To populate the world. To me, this directive is logical. We need a man and woman to come together to make children, right? So, in terms of increasing in number and filling the earth this was a sensible suggestion for humanity. It was also a wise recommendation for humanity to care for the earth we were going to live on. Caring for the earth would help us survive and populate.

Now… drum roll please… Let's connect those verses with the passage in Revelation where we imagine a resplendent Holy City filled with billions, maybe trillions, or an inconceivable number of people… If God, in his imagination before the creation of the world, had a picture of this vast quantity of people, it makes perfect sense that his first instruction was to populate the earth. But that wasn't the whole story, because God's image of heaven isn't just about having masses of people to live with forever…

**It's about having masses of people who**
**love *God and love one another* for eternity.**
**Can you imagine *that*?**

"How do we get there?" I'm so glad you asked.

This is where Jesus' new mandate comes in…

# Chapter 11
# AN INVITATION TO LOVE

Jesus came to earth and represented God perfectly. He spent three years teaching people to weave a covering of love. When we embrace his teaching, everything we do, the things we say, and the decisions we make become a beautifully woven life of love.

Jesus showed us what love looks like by dying for us and what resurrection life means by rising from the dead. ONLY then did he say, "Ok, you're ready for my new mandate. I've got something else for you."

This is what he said:

> **Mark 16:15:** "Go into all the world and preach the gospel to all creation."

What a huge instruction! But what does it mean? And is it still relevant?

In this verse, Jesus used the word 'all' twice: all the world and all creation. It sounds like an enormous task! Before we look at how expansive the mandate is, I'd like to focus on the phrase in the middle: 'preach the gospel'. Christians throughout the centuries have taken the word 'preach' and expressed the account of Jesus in diverse ways from home gatherings to cathedrals, from proclaiming on street corners to tv evangelism, from quiet coffee shop conversations to massive, stadium-filled rallies. The idea behind the word 'preach' is to make Jesus known. Why? Because the gospel is the good news of who Jesus is, what he has accomplished for us, and the incredible difference that his presence makes in our daily lives.

"Extra! Extra! Read all about it!" This was a familiar cry in the early 1900s as vendors attempted to sell their newspapers with urgent bulletins. The word 'preach' in Greek is 'kérussó'; meaning to publicly proclaim or announce something, usually of vital importance. Whilst we may critique the different methods that have been used to share the gospel, (which we will look at in Chapter 13) the intent has been, in most cases, to let the world know that Jesus offers hope to a broken world through the message he shared.

- Jesus' message to restore the broken relationship humanity has with God is love.
- Jesus' message to restore the fractured relationships we have with one another is love.
- Jesus' message to heal our emotional wounds and find restoration for our hearts in a hurt-filled world is love.

LOVE is the good news. It is designed to help individuals, families, communities, and even nations flourish. Its intention is the well-being of humanity and the beautiful planet we live on. In the original mandate, God blessed the union of a man with his wife who were to populate the earth for the purpose of creating flourishing communities who nurture the earth, for the prosperity of all. The *intent* of that original mandate remains, but Jesus expands its meaning to include his teaching about love.

## AN INVITATION TO LOVE

**Love is the purpose of it all and how it is accomplished.**

**What Jesus asked his disciples to 'preach' is an invitation for people to live in a connected, intimate relationship with God, in which they lovingly care for their authentic selves, from which they love others with the capacity they have.**

This invitation is still available and relevant to us today. When we accept this invitation, we are choosing to live by faith, believing that this way of life (living by love) is in our best interests, and in the best interests of others. From this perspective, we become intrinsically motivated to care about the wellbeing of those around us. We want them to flourish.

**Living the law of love is the most effective way to preach the gospel, because we are communicating by our actions that God's ways are trustworthy and for our good. We don't need a microphone to preach. We simply need to love, and if anyone asks us why, we point them to Jesus, who taught us how to love in the first place.**

This has significant implications for how we live. We can ask ourselves questions like:

- Do the choices I make keep me healthy, protect my heart, nourish my mind, keep me well…? Do my choices help *me* flourish?
- Do the things that I say and the way that I treat others help *them* flourish? Am I concerned about *their* wellbeing in my decision-making?
- Are the activities I do helpful in building meaningful relationships in my family and friendship groups? Are my contributions helping *my community* flourish?

- Are my spending habits wise, not just in looking after myself or my family, but helpful to those who produced the items, like those working in factories or coffee plantations, etc.? What are the long-term, world-wide implications of my choices? Am I helping *my world* to flourish?
- Are the goods I'm consuming sustainable, re-usable, recyclable, renewable? Are my choices ethical? Are they helpful to *my planet* flourishing?

These are personal, individual questions but could easily be applied to workplaces, communities, organisations, and nations using the same principle: Is this decision helping create a better world, or am I harming it? This is the implementation of good stewardship.

The biggest barrier to fulfilling the law of love is self-interest. Self-interest is very different to self-care. Maintaining personal boundaries and looking after our own wellbeing is self-care. There is nothing wrong with wanting good things for ourselves. Every good thing we get to enjoy is a gift from God. (James 1:17) Self-interest, however, is caring about what we want *without* caring how our decisions impact others around us. It is an entitled, proud attitude where we take what we want, regardless of the consequences.

Power, wealth, and position are used for personal gain, not only to the detriment of others, but often deliberately hurting others in the process. We see this at work where people are exploited, in human trafficking, in domestic violence, in how refugees are treated, how workers are misused, how the marginalised are rejected. We see it in the way we treat our planet... All over our world we see the effects of the absence of love. Intrinsically, we know it's harmful. Yet the insatiable drive for wanting what *we* want, without considering the impact it may have on those (and the world) around us, overrides the law of love. We choose to not trust God's ways. We sin.

Despite this, Jesus kindly keeps inviting us back to himself. There is always grace, acceptance, and forgiveness. He encourages us to reconsider our actions so that we can find ways to align our decisions, actions, goals, and plans with his law of love. When we do, not only are our own interests taken care of, but the things we do have a positive impact on those around us as well. As our hearts expand to encompass others, we find joy in seeing people thriving because of our choices. In this joy, *we* flourish.

Paul encourages his readers through his letter to the Philippians.

> **Philippians 2:3-5:** "Do nothing out of selfish ambition or vain conceit. Rather, in humility value others above yourselves, not looking to your own interests but each of you to the interests of the others. In your relationships with one another, have the same mindset as Christ Jesus…"

Paul went on to expand on how Jesus modelled this mindset in the way he demonstrated sacrificial love, in how he gave his own life for us. Whilst we don't always like to hear it, an important part of love is learning what times are appropriate to give up what we want and choose what may be in someone else's best interests instead. There is wisdom needed in this, but sacrificial love powerfully displays the character of Jesus. Like, rescuing someone in danger, giving up a seat on the train, offering to make a meal, providing a warm blanket… There are lots of opportunities to give selflessly to others.

Love isn't just a feeling or state of being. It's a verb, a *doing* word. It requires action. It also requires a recipient. We need someone to love. Just as God created us as human beings in his image to love, we, too, are created to love each other. This is why we have the potential to flourish in communities.

> **This is the purpose and the power of the church:
> We have the opportunity as a community
> of faith to be agents of God's love in a very
> muddy, broken, hurting world.**

Together, we can find ways to put God's love into action and encourage one another to keep loving, even in the face of opposition. We can keep each other accountable when our behaviour is harmful rather than wholesome. We can help one another re-think how we live so that the truth of Jesus stays relevant and mindful of the impact we are having – not just as individuals and families – but in our wider community and on this planet that we call home.

Now, there may be a query brewing in the back of your mind... I'm sure you know people who have no relationship with Jesus, nor connection with the church, that are doing amazing, loving, sacrificial work to positively impact the world. So... what is the difference between Christians coming up with plans for the good of humanity and people who aren't? Great question!

We are made in the image of God, designed to live by the law of love. It is instinctual, so it makes sense that any human being would have the capacity to love others and find ways to serve. There is humanitarian aid and kindness in action happening all around the world. Without even knowing it, they are operating in alignment with the law of love. Christianity merely acknowledges this as something that God, as our creator, has established as our original design, even when it might be considered foolish. We testify that this is God's will for humanity and that, by faith, living according to this design is the best way to live. We can affirm and collaborate with them in their efforts.

Embracing the law of love, following Jesus' example of compassion and generosity, has the unlimited power to transform lives and whole communities. When Jesus said, 'to all the world' and 'to all creation' I imagine that he wasn't thinking of one person with a big megaphone or, these days, someone being a world-wide influencer on the internet with millions of followers. Rather, I believe Jesus could envisage the collective impact we could achieve as his body, when we put our heads and hearts together and choose to find ways to demonstrate his love in a world that desperately needs his hope. The ripple effects of a simple act of love cannot be underestimated, nor the torrential current of an outpouring of love by a whole community.

Our time on this earth is limited. What matters the most? Is it our wealth, success, achievements? Or is it how well we have loved? I hope that when my time comes, I will be able to say, "With all my heart."

## Chapter 12

# OFFERING SOMEONE A BLANKET OF LOVE

All throughout Jesus' ministry and teaching he taught people to re-think their beliefs, offering them a central, common value on which to base their beliefs and enact their decisions: LOVE.

"Are you thinking about how you're loving yourself, God, and others?" That's the essence of the New Commandment. Jesus wasn't taking Old Testament scripture and trying to strictly impose its rules and laws. That's legalism. He was encompassing the legal system saying, "The point of the law is LOVE. Love is the overarching concept to embrace so that the things you do and say, based on your values and beliefs, are all done from a perspective of love."

> **Jesus wasn't teaching his followers to quilt a hodgepodge patchwork of rules and laws.**
> **He was teaching them to weave a life of faith, expressing itself in love. (Galatians 5:6b)**

## OFFERING SOMEONE A BLANKET OF LOVE

This is where the idea of the woven poncho came from. When we put on love, it covers so much of the muck of our world. Love enfolds us in a beautiful covering that embellishes our lives and motivates our hearts to act in good-faith and good-will towards others.

> **1 Peter 4:8:** "Above all, love each other deeply, because ***love covers*** over a multitude of sins." *(Bold and italics mine.)*

Let's think about weaving for a moment. Weaving draws threads together. As Christians, we use the loom of Jesus' death and resurrected life as a framework on which to weave the threads of our lives, creating unique patterns and symbols that reflect the unfolding story of our relationship with him.

When we weave, we can create pictures of the ways we express love. Some of us might be good listeners and encouragers. Others may be great gift givers or enjoy spending time with people. Some may be hospitable, generous, or helpful, whilst others are awesome huggers.

Regardless of the methods, what God looks at is our heart. (1 Samuel 16:7b) He sees the true motives that underlie our actions and is absolutely delighted when he recognises his heart of love in us. This is why self-love, in the context of a loving relationship with Jesus, is the beginning point on which to base the law of love. It is in that context that we can re-think our thinking, examine our motives, protect our hearts, find healing and wholeness, and be our truest, most authentic selves. It is *whilst* we are caring for ourselves, dealing with our own muddy issues, that we can offer Jesus' love to others.

God is interested in our wellbeing and wants us to flourish as authentic individuals, so we can offer our truest selves to the world from a place of self-accepting confidence, and wholehearted care. Jesus invites us to weave a life of love, seeing opportunities that may arise throughout our day where we can love others, with whatever capacity we have in that moment. Embracing the opportunity, we can wrap a blanket around someone who might need it at that moment.

Let me share a story with you.

I was in a small shopping centre to pick up some groceries. Before doing the shop, I went to the bathroom and was at the basin when a lady walked in. I could see that she was upset. Something in me stirred. Was that me or was it the Holy Spirit? I don't know, but I needed to say something, so I simply asked, "Are you all right?"

The lady replied, "No." She then shared her story.

She'd been sitting at a café having a coffee when she'd been approached by a couple of friends whom she hadn't seen in ages. She said it was lovely to see them and good to catch up. Then they asked her how her husband was, and she told them that he had recently passed away. She was so sad to have to keep telling people over and over. And she was there, at the shopping centre, doing grocery shopping for one, and had to go home to an empty house – alone.

She began to sob. At that moment, all I could do was wrap a figurative blanket of love around her. I gave her a hug and held her whilst she cried. Time stood still and the moment lingered as she poured out her grief. I didn't have to say anything or follow her up. There was nothing spiritual about that moment. We were in a bathroom of all places! Yet that moment was *everything* spiritual, because in that moment I got to be Jesus to her and wrap *his* arms around her and hold her, wrap *his* blanket of love around her and comfort her in that place.

There are opportunities for expressions of love all throughout our day if we're willing to see them. Life is full of distractions and lists of things to do, so love can require intentional focus and a heart that is looking out for the wellbeing of others. In essence, it's meaningfully connecting with people, for the purpose of making their lives better. In making that choice, we are also making our communities stronger. In other words, we are helping them flourish.

> **True love is walking alongside other
> people, *wherever we* are,
> loving them *as they* are.**

We know we are loving well when we see the effects (or fruit) of our actions. (Matthew 7:17-18, John 13:35, Galatians 5:22-23) People are encouraged and edified. They experience freedom to be authentic and live as unique individuals, marvellously made by God. There is a sense of connection and collaboration. There is support and care. There is vision, hope, joy, and oodles of grace.

This doesn't mean that we always get it right. Despite good intentions, people can still misinterpret our actions and get offended, uncomfortable, or even outraged. Let's face it, communication is tricky, and what we say or do may not be the message people receive. This is why learning to communicate clearly is one of the most valuable skills we can acquire.

Love isn't 'me-centred'. Its focus is on others. It is free of judgement. Love releases us from comparisons about whose sin is worse, because as human beings we are all stuck in the mud, covered in it, contaminated by it. No mud is worse than any other mud. Mud is mud.

We're all in the same predicament. Sure, some actions have far worse consequences than others, but in the end we all wrestle with the same stuff. This is how we have the potential to forgive with compassion. I'm not saying that's a simple or easy thing to do. Far be it! It can be one of the hardest things to do, and it is a process that can take a long time. Sometimes, we don't get there. We simply walk away.

Forgiveness is a central theme throughout the Bible, epitomised by Jesus' demonstration of love on the cross, as we discussed in Chapter 7. His example of forgiveness is our model for forgiving others.

> **Ephesians 4:32:** "Be kind and compassionate to one another, forgiving each other, just as in Christ God forgave you."

This model is not excusing or justifying bad behaviour. It also doesn't disregard the consequences of hurtful actions. Forgiveness is not a *feeling* that we can somehow generate.

**Forgiveness is a decision that chooses to release someone into God's hands without seeking revenge.**

In that release, we free ourselves from vindictive thoughts. We intentionally choose not to store the memory of their behaviour in our mental arsenal of wrongdoings to use against the person in the future. This includes not gossiping to others about what the person has done. It also means choosing to forgive that person every time they, or the event that caused harm, comes to mind. That can mean a LOT of forgiveness over a LONG period. (Matthew 18:22)

Whilst we might feel the sting of injustice when something harmful is done to us, when we entrust someone into God's hands, we trust that *his* justice will ultimately be accomplished. To believe in God's perfect justice, and especially the timing of it, takes faith.

Letting go through forgiveness gives us freedom to move on. It helps us look for constructive pathways to right wrongs and create spaces where we can have compassionate conversations with one another to understand why someone may have acted in a certain way. This has the potential to provide an opportunity for them to consider how their actions have hurt God, themselves, others, and their world. It gives them an opportunity to repent and change their behaviour. To love authentically, we need to have honest conversations with one another, especially if we're feeling hurt by someone else's behaviour. Because this is so important, I've dedicated a whole chapter to the topic. (See Chapter 17.)

When Jesus was asked by one of his disciples how to pray, he included in his prayer to "forgive us our sins, as we forgive those who sin against us". (Luke 11:1-4, Matthew 6:9-14) In practising forgiveness towards one another, we are also remembering that we, too, need forgiveness. We have our own muddy issues to deal with. There will be times where we need to ask for the forgiveness of others.

Giving a sincere apology is an important part of restoring a relationship. It takes humility to recognise that we've done something that has hurt someone, intentionally or even unintentionally. In saying sorry, we're acknowledging the importance of the relationship that we want to restore. We're also recognising that we have been re-thinking our actions and want to make amends. As we address whoever is involved, we need to specifically admit the things we have done that have been harmful and, as best we can, articulate how they may have negatively impacted the person or people involved. We need to be able to show how we are going to change our behaviour and ask for their forgiveness. We need to graciously give people time to consider our words and accept their response, regardless of what that may be, along with the consequences that may arise.

Restoration of damaged relationships can take time. It's not easy to believe in someone after trust has been broken, yet trust is what is required. Reconciliation is God's heart for us and the pathway he invites us to journey with him on. He went to enormous lengths to show how much he loves and forgives us, restoring the ka-thunk issue of our broken trust with him. He invites us to work on maintaining our relationships with others by showing people compassion, understanding, and grace, just as he does with us.

It should be noted that forgiveness and reconciliation are two different things. Forgiveness is the beginning point of restoring relationships and is a one-sided heart orientation that we can control. Reconciliation, however, requires both (or all) parties to have that same disposition and work together towards healing the relational fractures sustained. Sometimes, reconciliation isn't possible, even with complete forgiveness. There may be limits because of physical, emotional, or other necessary boundaries that need to be appropriately put in place, or consequences that protect others that need to be applied. It can be a muddy journey. So, get your gumboots ready!

And… just as we're getting our heads around the complexities of forgiveness, we discover that Jesus rose the bar and showed us how to extend love even further…

In establishing the law of love as the highest value to aspire to, Jesus raised the bar of expectation not just from loving those who have hurt or offended us, but to extend love even to our enemies. (Matthew 5:43-48, Luke 6:27) This invitation wasn't just to offer our enemies forgiveness, but to wish them well. An even higher bar than that is to wish them so much wellness that they find an abundant, flourishing, thriving life with Jesus. Are we willing to do *that*?

Just as the bar of loving is extended to reach higher in loving others, it is also extended inwardly in loving ourselves. Self-forgiveness, learning to love ourselves through our mistakes and failures, is a tough challenge. How often do I beat myself up for the things I've done? How often do I go round and around in the washing machine of thought of what I 'could have', 'should have', 'would have' done? I feel the stains of guilt and shame as I blame myself over and over again.

## OFFERING SOMEONE A BLANKET OF LOVE

I have to keep remembering that Jesus' handwoven blanket covers me. It covers my past errors and wrongdoings. God still loves me unconditionally and reminds me that 'as far as the east is from the west' he has taken my sins away. (Psalm 103:12) As an all-knowing God, it is impossible for him to forget my sins, rather, he *chooses* to not remember them. (Hebrews 8:12, Isaiah 43:25) In other words, he has decided not to think about them at all and treat me as though they never happened. When I believe this, I can gracefully practise self-forgiveness, stop the washing machine and hang those thoughts out to dry, re-examining them in the light of God's truth and what *he* says of me, rather than what I think of myself. (This is part of the process of re-thinking about thinking.) From there, I can receive his forgiveness, start fresh, and live in faith, believing that I am still loved and accepted by God – no matter what.

As we love ourselves, we can love others. Self-love includes self-forgiveness. Self-forgiveness expands our compassion towards others because we can appreciate that they, too, struggle with self-worth and dealing with *their* muddy issues. (Ephesians 4:32) This expands our vision to look for those who are hurting or struggling and could use a hand. We intentionally begin to seek out people to whom we can offer a woven blanket of love.

Just as in our story the bride began to get a little overwhelmed with the size of the task of handing out blankets to everyone, the groom gave her a suggestion to simplify the process, making the task more doable. He simply said, "Just start with one." The way we change our world is by one act of loving kindness at a time.

Who will you find to love today?

# Part 5
# THE PARTNERSHIP

# THE BRIDEGROOM'S WOVEN BLANKET

*Scene 5*

United in purpose, with the heart of wanting to help each guest reach the bridegroom, the bride and the guest planned to help those struggling through the mud. The bride went back to get more blankets. The guest went to support those who were walking.

Miraculously, the blanket gave them strength and determination to carry out their tasks with ease and efficiency. Because they were non-stick, the woven blankets enabled them to move through the mud so much more quickly. Oh. The effort and straining, how hard *that* had been! Now, they felt lighter, happier. They discovered their steps were firmer, more resolved. They realised they were stronger than they knew. They smiled at each other across the mud.

More and more guests arrived. Laughter and hugs abounded, as new guests put on their own, personalised, woven blankets. There was a collective sense of togetherness because they were all in the same sticky situation, trying to help one another wade through the muck.

The more guests that arrived, the more effectively they were able to help one another through the mud because they *collaborated*. Getting to the wedding was the goal. Coming alongside each other and sharing the load was the method.

They began to construct ways to make the journey to the church more efficient. There were plans of building bridges over the deep parts, and boardwalks over the shallower ones. They made warning signposts for pitfalls and dangers along the way. They became creative problem-solvers, finding camaraderie in working through the issues that presented themselves.

It seemed to be working out seamlessly.

But mud has a habit of getting messy, *very* quickly.

Yes, those muddy conditions were far from perfect. People began venting their frustrations about their mucky circumstances. People got tired, grumpy, and annoyed with each other. Some people imposed harsh methods of how to do things and got impatient when the outcomes weren't successful, or tasks were taking too long. People divided into groups and became increasingly exclusive as to whom they would allow to join. Some groups became territorial and would only help people who came into *their* area. Some groups refused to collaborate, even though they had the same mission and plenty of resources to share. Yes, at times, working in the mud made people stubborn, ungracious, and hurtful. After all, underneath their blankets they were still wearing muddy clothes.

Inevitably, disputes arose about how to best help people in the mud. Some disagreements were about methodology in muddy issues. Some were about who the bridegroom is and the kinds of guests he would invite. Some were about the roles they each had. Other times it was about leadership. They tried hard to solve these problems, but when disputes couldn't be resolved, some guests would go their separate ways and help people in other areas. Sadly, others gave up. That was the nature of working with people in muddy conditions.

To help, the bridegroom offered to teach the guests how to weave additional layers into their woven blankets and help patch relationships back together again. These layers included forgiveness, grace, acceptance, respect, inclusion, support, wisdom, and patience. He invited them to consider how to find loving ways of supporting one another in their sticky messes.

The bridegroom taught the guests how to create environments that were healthy and safe, where people could heal from the wounds they'd sustained whilst traipsing through the mud. These spaces gave people reprieve from trudging. They offered places where they could simply *'be'* and breathe. They provided areas of contemplation, so guests could consider how to look after themselves better in the process. They offered encouragement to keep working at their tasks whilst making wiser choices in their methods.

The bridegroom dedicated time to each guest, loving them in their own unique way, appreciating their contribution to solving muddy issues, and enabling them to find purposeful ways of not just getting through the mud, but learning to *thrive* in it. His words gave his guests confidence and grace, fresh ideas and genius solutions, motivation, stamina and, above all, hope. He kept reminding them that this wasn't the end, that what was to come would be more incredible than they ever dared to dream or imagine. His enthusiasm was contagious. His support was unfailing. His love was unending.

He kept reminding the guests of how much he appreciated every one of them by continuing to weave unique patterns into their stunningly crafted blankets that they wore with gratitude. In wearing them, they knew they belonged with the bridegroom and his bride and that, one day, a celebration would come that would leave all this muddy muck as a dim memory…

## Chapter 13
# COVERING OR SMOTHERING

"**G**o into all the world." Go is a 'doing' word. It's action. In this case, **it is love in motion.** As we discussed in Chapter 11, the new mandate Jesus offered to his followers is a calling to love so that we can flourish as individuals and communities living on this beautiful planet.

In the book of Matthew, this mandate appears with a different set of instructions. It has the same heart and purpose but uses different wording. Let's look.

> **Matthew 28:19-20:** "Go and make disciples of all nations, baptising them in the name of the Father and of the Son and of the Holy Spirit, and teaching them to obey everything I have commanded you. And surely I am with you always, to the very end of the age."

'Go'… 'make disciples'… 'baptise'… 'teach'…

These were Jesus' instructions, given moments before he ascended to heaven. By this stage, Jesus must have felt that his disciples were ready to receive them – or as prepared as they ever would be.

We summarise these instructions by calling them 'discipleship'. We can be a disciple, which is what we refer to as our individual relationship with Jesus and how we follow his example. We can also make disciples which is how we encourage others to follow him. One of the most pertinent questions we can ask as Christians is, "How do we make disciples through the perspective of 'faith expressing itself through love?'"

I was blessed to grow up in a family that not only has a genuine heart for God, but a purposeful heart for mission. In fact, my parents took these verses and concept of discipleship quite literally and flew our family to live in the coldest, windiest, southernmost city in the world: Punta Arenas, Chile. My parents weren't sent as a part of a missionary organisation. They simply felt called by God to go. So we went, believing that this is what we were meant to do, and where we were meant to go, at that stage of our lives. They were formative years and I'm grateful for the experience and the lifelong friendships I formed.

Over time, I've done some re-thinking about what discipleship means, especially in terms of evangelism and mission. I've had to ask what's been helpful and what's harmful? Am I *covering* someone graciously with a blanket of Jesus' love (allowing them to freely breathe in his life-giving Spirit), or am I *smothering* them in the process (i.e. sucking the life out of them)? What does it mean to be a follower of Jesus that truly serves other people graciously, with compassion and kindness? In other words, what methods of sharing the good news about Jesus **are the most loving**?

By putting discipleship into my pensieve, I have a fresh perspective, which I've distilled into two categories: what discipleship is and what discipleship isn't. Hopefully this will help clarify what discipleship may or may not be; what could be useful or, dare I say it, downright harmful. I reiterate that this is *my* distilling of ideas. You don't have to agree with me. Please just keep an open mind.

Let's start with **what discipleship ISN'T:**

1. To me, discipleship isn't about **SAVING PEOPLE.** Everything that was needed for the salvation of humanity was accomplished through the death of Jesus on the cross and his resurrection. Full stop. (See Chapter 7.) Therefore, our mandate isn't to go about saving people. It's not to rescue people. That's God's job.

2. Discipleship is also not about **CONVERTING PEOPLE.** The idea of imposing a religious system on people and telling them what and how they must think dismisses that Jesus came to teach us *how to love* and *that faith is all about a relationship with him*. Conversion is like asking people to conform to *our interpretation* of how religion 'should' be. It ungraciously demands that people say the 'sinner's prayer' to 'cross the line' so that they're 'in'. It's a numbers-focused approach rather than a loving, relational approach, usually linked to saving souls. I'm not saying that repentance isn't important. Far be it! This book is about repentance. But it is Jesus, in the context of a loving relationship with us, who saves us and changes us. Jesus helps us to re-think about thinking, which informs our beliefs and changes our actions. It is not a legalistic, religious system demanding conformity.

3. It follows, then, that discipleship is not about **CHANGING PEOPLE.** When people come to discover a personal relationship with Jesus, it is not our mandate to demand that they change who they are. It's not our job to say, "You need to be *this* (whatever our *'this'* is)." Seriously, how dare we compel people to change based on

what *we* think they should be or how they should behave, when they should change or the order they should change in? If we try to change people, we are assuming we know what's best for them, according to *our* viewpoint, theology, and life experience. That's a very arrogant position to put ourselves in, and a very ungracious way of treating other people. Change is the work of the Holy Spirit. We can come alongside people and support them in the work that God is doing in them. I don't believe it's up to us to tell people that they must change to be acceptable to God, approved by him, or loved by him. They already are. So are we, even in our muddied state. That's what grace is.

Over decades of church life and seeing Christianity in action, I've found that these approaches to discipleship have been more harmful than helpful. I've witnessed a lot of people hurt and leave the church because we have gone about discipleship with the right heart of wanting people to know Jesus, yet with an unhelpful approach. I've been guilty of these methods and mindsets myself. You only know what you know, right? This was what I was brought up to believe and I sincerely thought it was my responsibility to save the world.

Can you identify with any of these approaches? How do *you* view discipleship?

If the previous three approaches are unhelpful, what *is* going to be helpful in showing people God's love and inviting them into a relationship with Jesus? I went back to the scriptures to find some answers.

1. Discipleship is about **BEING A WITNESS**.

**Acts 1:8:** "You will receive power when the Holy Spirit comes on you; and you will be my witnesses in Jerusalem, and in all Judea and Samaria, and to the ends of the earth."

This verse describes discipleship from the perspective of expanding influence; Jerusalem – Judea – Samaria – ends of the earth. If we put those places in concentric circles in our world today it would be like saying, "You will be my witnesses in your homes, with your neighbours, in your workplaces, in your communities… and to the ends of the earth." Wherever we are, wherever we go, we can be witnesses of Jesus' love. We can BE LOVE. And remember, it's not that we, ourselves, *must* go all over the world. Some of us might, but most of us won't. 'To the ends of the earth' implies the potential that the ripple effects our loving actions can have.

What is a witness? In a courtroom, a witness testifies to what they've seen with their own eyes. For me, as a witness, I'm testifying to the truth of what God has done in my life. Here are just some of the many ways I can testify about Jesus and the difference having a faith in God has made in my life.

- I can testify that having a living faith in Jesus gives me a real sense of **purpose**. Loving God and loving others is purposeful. It gives me a reason to get up in the morning and how to focus my time and energy each day.
- Faith also gives me a huge sense of **community**. Being part of a church community, both locally and with the wider community of faith, gives me a sense of belonging. I can contribute my skills and abilities. I can practise love. I can

also ask for help and support in times when life is challenging. This makes a HUGE difference in my life.
- I can testify to God's **provision** in my life. God has provided me with friends and family, a home, employment, food I enjoy, and a reliable vehicle… There is SO much to be grateful for. I can specifically testify to God's financial provision. There have been many times when I've struggled to make ends meet and I've asked for God's help, and he has faithfully provided for my needs in unexpected ways. He also gives me the ability to earn money and budget carefully, along with a heart of stewardship and generosity to balance my finances.
- I can testify to God's **healing** in my life. I was supernaturally healed of post-natal depression after being prayed for, which I had experienced as a weight over me for four years. I can also testify to *not* being healed from fibromyalgia and managing it for nearly twenty years. In that, however, I can testify daily to God's grace and enabling to do the things I've *needed* to do (not necessarily all the things I've *wanted* to do) by re-adjusting expectations of myself, learning a whole lot more about God, and discovering unanticipated emotional healing in unexplored areas of my life. If you ask me which requires more faith, it would be in trusting God's daily provision of strength, courage, and grace for each day with chronic illness. I exercise that faith every morning I wake up.
- I can also testify to **reconciliation** in my life, particularly the restoration of a badly torn relationship with a family member. Praise God for that! The Holy Spirit's work in devastatingly fractured relationships, or the little micro-

tears which happen in everyday life, has kept so many of my relationships intact. He works through the application of Biblical wisdom in timely and relevant ways to fit each unique circumstance I face. I'm so grateful for the power of forgiveness and restoration in my life.

- Like many other Christians, I've learned to live with the tension of God's wondrous provision in **answered prayer,** and the uncertainty and confusion of prayers left unanswered, or certainly unanswered in the way I had hoped or expected. Having to trust God's faithfulness and character in the silence is one of the biggest challenges to my faith, yet one of the greatest times of personal growth. This is when I've learned to hold on to his Word, even when I can't see a way ahead. In essence, I've learned to walk by faith, not by sight. (2 Corinthians 5:7)

By being a witness to the impact Jesus has made in our lives, we are showing people what life with him looks like. We are introducing them to someone who will accept and welcome them as they are, partner with them in life, and give them hope and purpose for their future. The story of our walk with Jesus can make a big difference in allowing someone to appreciate the wonderful experience exploring a life of faith can bring.

There are many other things I could testify about God's sustaining presence in my life, and even each of these points have tons of stories I could share. We each have a story. What's *your* story? What would *you* testify about if someone asked you how Jesus makes a difference in *your* life?

Let's think about this more broadly. When we come together in our little home groups or larger church gatherings, we bring our communal stories together, which create a collective story about what God is doing amongst us. How cool is *that*?

Now, let's expand that idea even further and re-examine the picture in Revelation 21… I get goosebumps thinking about this! Imagine that vast number of billions upon billions, maybe trillions, maybe *ZILLIONS* of people of all humanity, from all the ages, bringing their collective stories, all testifying to God's grace in their lives… How amazing is that! THIS is the story of humanity that we will take with us into eternity. WOW!

2. Discipleship is about **REPRESENTING JESUS**.

   **1 Peter 2:12:** "Live such good lives… (that) …they may see your good deeds and glorify God." *(Abbreviated)*

Just like a sporting team wears a uniform and represents a club, we represent Jesus and his kingdom. We wear the team colours of the character of God and the values of his kingdom. I confess that I don't always do a good job of this. In fact, I stuff up quite regularly. To keep my heart and actions in check it's good to be reminded I am representing Jesus. My actions reflect on him and may either bring people closer to knowing who Jesus is or turn them away.

Remember in Chapter 9, we talked about the beginnings of faith and how our understanding and experience of God determines how we respond to him? How many people have been turned off from being in a relationship with Jesus because they have been abused, harshly treated, or even discarded by the church? How that must break God's heart.

The way we represent Jesus can be termed as our 'apostolic witness'. From the moment we engage with other human beings on any given day, we are being 'sent by God' (that's what it means to be an apostle) to love them. The question is: How well do we do this? Will my children know Jesus better by the way I've spoken to them today? Will my partner feel loved by how I choose to connect? Will I offer patience to the driver in front of me who is driving a car clearly marked 'Swift' but going SO SLOW!?

People see. They're watching. Am I modelling Jesus' love to them? My prayer is that I would increasingly be a better reflection of Jesus to the people in my world. And for all those times when I drop the ball - when I'm tired, irritable, frustrated, angry, upset… and say and do things that I wish I hadn't, that God's grace would be sufficient. I hope that someone else can pick up the ball and show love when I fail to. It's meant to be a team sport! There is incredible power when we band together and collectively show love. We can right injustices, feed the hungry, house the homeless, defend the beaten, heal the broken, and give hope to a world that so desperately needs it. That's the kind of team I want to be part of.

Baptism is a way of presenting that we are part of 'Team Jesus'. We put aside our old way of living (go under the water) and put on the new jersey, choosing to live for Jesus (coming up out of the water). I've chosen to represent this jersey as a woven blanket. We don't need to be baptised to be saved. Jesus has already done that. What we're recognising in baptism is that we are now part of a community – a team, which lives in a way that wants to represent Jesus to the best of our ability, carrying out his purpose for us to love him and one another as we love ourselves.

3. Lastly, discipleship is about **TEACHING OTHERS HOW TO LOVE**.

**John 13:35:** "By this everyone will know that you are my disciples, if you love one another."

Weaving a life of love is the ultimate way of displaying Jesus' love to the world. We weave a picture of Jesus by the way we weave our lives of love. That is how we affect our families, communities, and workplaces: By loving.

Teaching others to love, sharing our understanding of the Bible, and telling people what we know about Jesus is all based on love. People can sense when we're not acting in love. If our agenda is about how many we convert, or that people adhere to *our* way of doing things, we are being legalistic critics who judge, disapprove, and reject others. Shame, that. Love is bigger and better than our narrow tunnel-vision of the Bible.

Modelling Jesus is one way of teaching people about him. We also have churches, Bible Study groups, online forums, book clubs, social groups, and discussion groups (and many other forums) that help us learn about God and his kingdom. There are missionary training agencies, courses, universities, and theological colleges that instruct people about Jesus. Many of these instruct people how to teach others about Jesus. Any kind of growth in our understanding of God, Jesus, and the Bible is a worthy pursuit. Our own Bible study and meditation of the scriptures are incredibly valuable and life transforming. Learning about Jesus helps us align our hearts and minds with his and changes the way we live it out. It helps us re-think about thinking and then help others re-think their thinking in line with kingdom values.

> **A disciple is an apprentice. We come alongside one another as fellow learners with humility and open minds to see how we can positively help our world flourish through how we LOVE.**
> ***This* is the true nature of discipleship.**

Going back to our story, discipleship is about helping one another through the mud, creatively problem-solving how we can do this in the most loving way possible. Life's tough. The road can feel long, hard, and exhausting. Walking alongside each other helps lighten the load and find solutions to the challenges we face. Weaving a life of love gives us the opportunity to offer hope to others in the middle of all the muck.

## Chapter 14
# AN INTIMATE PARTNERSHIP

How do we make Jesus known in a LOVING WAY? It's quite possible the disciples were wondering the same thing, yet Jesus already had the solution. Just before he ascended into heaven, Jesus gave his followers clear instructions. I'll paraphrase Jesus' words from Acts 1:8. He said, "Wait. Stay in Jerusalem. Don't go anywhere or start anything. I have something to give you that you're going to need. When you receive it… THEN you can go and be my witnesses." What was this gift? His Spirit.

We need the empowering of God's Holy Spirit, because let's face it, none of us can be all-loving all the time. We need God's help.

Receiving the Holy Spirit is like being given a special box full of amazing things. We're not going to unpack them all now because that isn't the scope and purpose of this book. However, they are worth a mention because they are incredible, and worth exploring in and of themselves.

Here are some examples of aspects of the Holy Spirit we can unwrap and discover:

- Spiritual gifts, like teaching, administration, evangelism, pastoring, service…
- 'Miraculous' spiritual gifts, like healing, speaking in tongues, signs, and wonders…
- Prophecy
- Words of knowledge
- How the Holy Spirit makes us holy (sanctification)
- Wisdom
- Being 'led' by the Spirit
- The 'fruit' of the Spirit
- Spiritual warfare
- Prayer and intercession
- Dreams and visions
- And much, much more…!

Each of us will react differently to the above, largely based on the teaching and experiences we've had. Some won't want to look at any of them, others will want to unpack all of them, whilst others might like to pick and choose or prioritise. Regardless of how we feel about the Holy Spirit and how he interacts in our lives, he is part of the Christian experience. We receive the salvation of Jesus and we're given the gift of the Holy Spirit. (Ephesians 1:13-14) The Holy Spirit is the essence of God in spirit form. It's a package deal. (Romans 8:9)

Our approach to the Holy Spirit is largely influenced by the teaching we've received and our experience in seeing him in action. If these have been edifying and have served to strengthen our faith and those of our faith-community, then we're likely to want to explore more of how the

Holy Spirit works. Sadly, however, I have seen aspects of the Holy Spirit's work that have not been managed well. Even when well-intentioned, misuse of scripture and unwise (or downright dishonest) handling of the supernatural can be damaging to faith, including turning people away who may be seeking Jesus and often deeply hurting them in the process.

For example, when we tell someone that they haven't been healed by God because of their lack of faith or their sins, we are saying the healing depends on *them,* rather than God. Yet, if healing is the work of the Holy Spirit, isn't it God's discretion how he chooses to work, even if we don't like or understand it? (Isaiah 40:28) As I mentioned earlier, I was healed supernaturally from depression yet allowed to live with chronic illness. Was I not healed of fibromyalgia because of my lack of faith? I don't think so. That would be damaging to my relationship with God, because it would all be up to me, and my efforts fell short. If it's all up to God, then I accept his choice for me by faith, appreciating that his thoughts are higher and wiser than mine. (Isaiah 55:8-9) I don't have to have all the answers as to 'why', but I can learn to trust him in not knowing. This increases my faith.

Recently I was in a terrible vehicle accident that crushed the left side of my body. Was God not protecting me? Of course he was! It could have been so much worse. Could he have healed me supernaturally? Of course! Yet sometimes he allows us to walk (or in this case, limp) through difficult things and gives us courage, strength, and grace to face each day, no matter how much pain we are going through. He also gives us a family of faith to love and care for us along the way. Bad things happen to good people. Bad things happen to Christian people.

> **Being a Christian does not make us immune to life's struggles and the problems of mud in this world.**

> **What God's Holy Spirit does is empower
> us each day to walk *through* them.**
> (Ephesians 3:16-17a)

The importance of mentioning the Holy Spirit and the incredible gift he is, is simply to say that there is so much to discover and explore. We are going to put those back in the box for now with two little mentions:

1. All these things about the Holy Spirit are probably not as mystical and 'woo-woo' as we may have been taught.
2. We can have all the gifts of the Spirit in the world, and we can see and experience incredible supernatural manifestations, but if we don't have love, they're not worth very much. In 1 Corinthians 13:1 Paul describes having supernatural empowerment without love like a 'clanging cymbal'. It's loud, unwanted noise, rather than beautiful, harmonious music.

Let's return to the bridegroom, because the empowering by the Holy Spirit is all about a loving partnership. It's like when two people come together. They have a beautiful relationship that grows as they cultivate it with time and commitment and dedicate themselves to one another. This becomes an interwoven life; so interwoven that sometimes you don't even know whose idea something was. "Was that your idea or was that my idea? Who knows? Who cares?! It doesn't matter!" Because you're doing it together, there's a wonderful sense of fulfilment in being one in heart, mind, and purpose. (Philippians 2:2) This is communion, which we celebrate and commemorate as we weave our lives together.

In my example of embracing a lady in a shopping centre bathroom, I felt like I needed to ask her if she was all right. Was that my idea or the

Holy Spirit moving my heart towards her? Who knows? The fact is, in an interwoven life with God's Holy Spirit we work in partnership.

> **The essence of discipleship is a loving partnership with Jesus, connecting with his heart, seeing people with his eyes of love, and offering that love to others in whatever way we can. It includes allowing space in our lives to expect the unexpected, because we never know what might happen or who we might meet in our day.**

Expecting the unexpected is like having cameras at the ready at a wedding. It's unpredictable, exciting, and messy at the same time, yet that is what the freedom of discipleship brings, for 'where the Spirit of the Lord is, there is freedom.' (2 Corinthians 3:17) The Holy Spirit gives us freedom to love generously and authentically without a sense of compulsion or obligation. There are no rules or formulas we must adhere to. We can be creative and have fun, finding ways of surprising people with love.

Law-abiding rule keepers like delineating life into clean-cut choices of 'right or wrong', 'do or don't'. This way they can keep people 'in or out', creating barriers, admonishing disapproval, and administering punishment if they don't keep the rules. Yet Jesus offered his followers a new way to re-think their thinking. He turned things upside down, inside out, and round about. Instead of providing clear regulations, he invited people to consider the guideline of LOVE.

The apostle Paul articulated the parameters of the law of love succinctly by saying that we have the right to do anything, but not everything is beneficial or constructive. (1 Corinthians 10:23) We have freedom to do *anything,* but with the law of love we have the ***responsibility*** to consider how we use that freedom to benefit ourselves, God, and others, and by extension, our communities, nation, and world. This includes looking at both the short-term and long-term implications of each decision we make. In using this directive, we can no longer look at all situations as equal and apply the same strategies and formulas in a 'one size fits all' approach. What Jesus did was to make things intricately complicated and frustratingly unclear, because his strategy means examining EVERYTHING through the lens of love, one choice at a time.

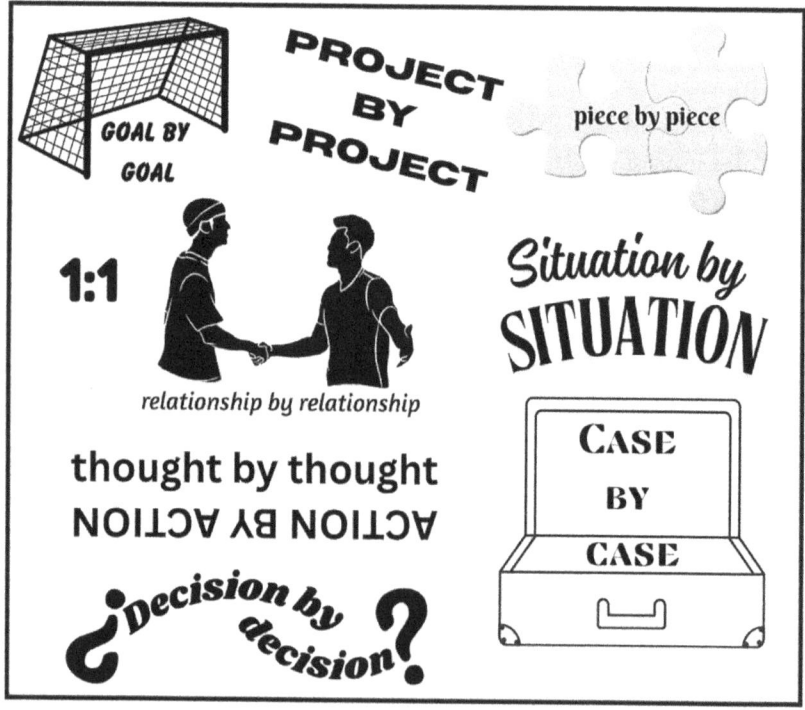

There are no pre-fixed ways of looking at problems. There are no 'have tos' or 'shoulds'. There are endless possibilities and a whole lot of freedom to make choices.

> Under the law of love, we have freedom
> with the *responsibility* to love.
> That is how Jesus loved.
> Let's call it loving freedom.

Loving freedom breaks down barriers and self-protective walls that divide us. Loving freedom invites inclusion and embraces diversity. Loving freedom looks for ways to build connections rather than enforcing exclusions. Why? Because we are intentionally looking for ways to help each other flourish by the choices we make, Christian or not, *without* the agenda of trying to make someone become one.

Loving freedom is a three-fold weaving of others, ourselves, and God. It is like a three-stranded woollen thread that creates the intricate, marvellous, creative patterns that form the expression of love in our lives. Responsibility invites a *response*. It generously allows people to respond in their own way, in their own time. In weaving loving freedom, not only are *we* free to choose how we love, but we also allow *others* to be themselves, accepting their limitations and respecting their boundaries. It graciously gives people permission to make choices which may (or may not) be helpful and to learn from, and live out, the consequences of those choices.

In weaving loving freedom into our own lives, we make choices that are going to help us thrive as individuals by evaluating our actions in line with both the long and short-term impact they may have for our own good – physically, emotionally, psychologically, financially, relationally, etc.

Loving freedom also helps us assess our decisions in line with what is most loving towards God by asking, **"What is the most God-honouring thing I can do in this situation?"** Appreciating that our actions affect his reputation and how he is perceived is, perhaps, the most important question to ask, because if we find that what we're doing is God-honouring, we can be guaranteed that it will be good for ourselves and others too.

> **In terms of making Jesus known, we can ask,
> "How can I make Jesus inviting and
> make love worth choosing?"**

Making decisions through the lens of love will always be complicated on this side of heaven because we are imperfect people making imperfect choices. We all live in mud. Rather than aiming for perfect solutions, it may be wiser and more graceful if we ask, "What are the *most* loving choices we can make in *these* circumstances?"

In doing this, we are opening our minds to consider the wider context in which we're making these choices, such as:

- The imperfect world we live in, with imperfect people
- The culture or nation we're part of and the governance we're living under
- Geopolitics and economic climate
- Organisational structures and systems
- The limitations of our resources
- The timeframe required
- The information and knowledge available
- Our understanding of someone's life experiences
- Appreciating each other's unique personalities
- Beliefs and personal values
- Our understanding of God at the time

I'm sure you can think of others.

In short, we are called to do the best we can at the time, within the context that we find ourselves. This often includes weighing up a whole range of imperfect solutions choosing the least damaging option, or the one with the least harmful consequences. This is why we write lists of pros and cons. It's essentially the same process. We'll never get it perfectly right, but God knows our heart and sees our motivations and that's what counts the most, because they will determine *how* we put those choices into action. How we enact our choices will either build or break relationships.

Because we're all in this muddy mess, Jesus has given us the task of re-connecting with one another when relationships inevitably get broken. This mandate in connectivity is what Paul calls the 'ministry of reconciliation'. (2 Corinthians 5:18-19) Loving freedom is the vehicle by which we implement it or, in the context of this book, the thread by which we weave it.

This reconciling work reflects what Jesus came to do through his death and resurrection. Jesus came to solve our mud problem by absorbing all of humanity's muddiness before God as he endured crucifixion. He died, and in his death all the broken trust was dealt with so faith could be restored. This is what we do with each other. Each time trust is broken between us, we work towards restoring it.

Through his resurrection, Jesus demonstrated the new life we can have throughout eternity with him. It is a long-term, permanent solution with a new life, a new creation, a new order of things. For now, however, our task is to learn to maintain relationships despite life's grubbiness.

We can learn to be inclusive and accept one another without judgement. We can practise offering forgiveness when people make mistakes. We can choose the interests of others over self-interest. We can discover fulfillment in following Jesus' example of loving, sacrificial service.

Jesus' call to his disciples is the same as his call to us today: "FOLLOW ME. Be my apprentice. Learn from my example." Jesus wove a life of love by living in an intimate partnership with his Father, empowered by the

Holy Spirit. He spoke his Father's words and enacted his Father's will. (John 5:19, 7:16, 12:49) He generously gave of himself for the benefit of those around him, with a long-term goal in mind: US. The collective US. All of US. Loving him and loving one another – forever.

Jesus has shown us how. Now we need to give it a go. Practise. Practise in the power of the Holy Spirit, like Jesus. Yes, it's not easy living with other people, but Jesus lived with *us!* In fact, he became one of us so we could live with him for eternity. In Hebrews 12:2, we are told that it was 'for the joy set before him' that Jesus endured the cross. What could that picture have been that gave him joy? Maybe, the image of the bridegroom with his bride; countless numbers of people loving him and loving each other forever. He saw it. He made it possible. Now we get to practise living it.

How that finds expression in each of our lives will depend on what passions, interests, gifts, and skills he has given us, and how we partner with him in his ministry of reconciliation. This can take so many forms: seeking justice, loving service, or healing broken relationships. It could be in caring for the environment and encouraging communities to be good stewards of earth. It could include fighting against human trafficking, finding help for those discriminated against and wronged, or providing practical help to those in need. It will mean remembering the poor, destitute, and marginalised. The ways we can love are infinite. The world-wide hardships are desperate. We simply need to ask Jesus, "How can we partner with you in showing your love today?"

In our purposeful acts of freely loving others, we weave those threads into the fabric of our life's story. As human beings created in God's image, we are his image-bearers to the world. Representing Jesus powerfully shows people who haven't had an encounter with him yet that they, too, reflect the character and kingdom of God. They have the capacity for love, kindness, goodness, patience, and helpfulness. When we identify the qualities of heaven in each other, we magnify them, praise them, and strengthen our own resolve to keep living out those values, building our communities on the incredible power that comes from love.

## Chapter 15

# A BLANKET OF HEALING

I wish this chapter was unnecessary.

I pre-empt it with a trigger warning for those who have been hurt in any way by someone professing to be a Christian, a church community, or a religious institution.

At heart, I am an idealist. I have a vision for the church where children can grow up in wholesome, safe, faith-based communities, being embraced as their authentic selves. It is a hope of creating spaces where people can cultivate their personal relationships with Jesus and learn to maintain healthy relationships with each other, and where individuals have the freedom to serve wholeheartedly using their abilities and resources, with whatever capacity they choose. I also believe in flourishing communities that welcome people who have never experienced what faith is about and allow them, at their own pace, in their own way, to discover purpose and passion in life with Jesus.

Sadly, the heartbreaking reality is that many people attend (and then leave) churches with emotional scars from some form of spiritual abuse, either through the structures of the institutions we fabricate, the harsh doctrine we promote, or the methodologies we implement. The fact is that, instead of finding a place where people can flourish, they discover inequality, judgement, control, manipulation, greed, and misuse of power imbalances. People walk away with deep wounds.

I personally know people who have rejected faith and Jesus because they have been:

- Told they are not welcome because of their sexual preferences or gender identity.
- Prohibited to minister (or hold a certain position in the church) because they are female.
- Prayed for to change who they are as a person.
- Coerced into behaving a certain way and believing certain doctrines.
- Gossiped about.
- Obligated to contribute to church funds beyond their means.
- An observer (or victim of) the misuse of church finances including stealing, fraud, and extortion.
- Controlled or manipulated through fear by the leadership of the church using public shaming and slander.
- Exposed to harsh, fear-based doctrine.
- Convinced they are not good enough, worthy enough, or acceptable enough to participate in church life.
- Told that their lack of faith is keeping them unwell, poor, or stuck in their current circumstances.
- Under leadership who speak on behalf of God, as though their words are infallible.
- The victim of power imbalances used to manipulate or control their behaviour.

- Expelled by their community and not allowed to have any contact with family and friends who are still there.
- Witness to the Word and name of God being used to justify horrific acts of violence and abhorrent behaviour.
- Physically or sexually abused.
- Unheard when they have voiced concerns about issues arising in the church.

Sadly, this list could continue for many more pages.

My heart breaks when I think about the damage we have done to people whilst supposedly representing God. If any of these form part of your experience of Christianity and life in a faith-based community, I am truly, truly sorry.

## I would like to offer you Jesus' woven blanket of loving healing.

I appreciate that even the *idea* of Jesus may be repugnant to you. I get that you may never want to know about him ever again. I just want to tell you that he's not the one to blame. WE are. People are. Messed-up people living in a messed-up world. WE did this. WE hurt one another. WE need to take responsibility.

I pray that you will find healing from whatever it is that you've been through. If you have been hurt, please seek help. Talk with someone. Find a counsellor or psychologist. **There is a list of possible sources of help at the end of this book.** Healing is a process. It takes time, so take all the time you need. Sometimes, we can heal in the context of community. Other times, we need to walk away. Do whatever you need to find healing. Please, protect your heart.

No matter where you're at in the process of piecing together your broken heart, the beauty of Jesus is that he is always there. His love, compassion, healing, wisdom, care, guidance, and restoration are always available. He can help you through the most unimaginable, horrendous, painful experiences. Whilst we continually fail one another, his love never fails. (1 Corinthians 13:8a)

Discipleship is about building healthy, loving relationships. If this isn't happening, we need to question why. What are our real motives for doing what we're doing? Is there anything about our structures or systems that isn't gracious? What aspects of our community need addressing so they become more grace-filled? What methodologies are we using that are harmful or unwelcoming? Is what we're doing *and the way we're doing it* aligned with Jesus' law of love? Are people experiencing love by being in our community? How are we exercising loving freedom?

As we seek to welcome people from all walks of life, inevitably people will come bearing scars of spiritual wounds. The last thing we want to do is hurt them again. They need all the love, support, care, and compassion we can give them. So, how do we offer Jesus' love in safe spaces where they can heal and simply 'be'? How can we nurture them in such a way that they can, one day, flourish? How do we become restorative communities?

Allow me to offer some suggestions:

- A foundation value is humility. As apprentices (disciples) of Jesus we need to be willing to examine *why* we do what we do, along with *how* we do what we do. Intentionally forming processes of debriefing and reflection to examine how well things are working, and identifying areas where we're not loving graciously, could be useful. This is part of the accountability we have towards one another in living in community. Humility allows us to be open to new ideas, flexible to adapt to new methods, teachable to re-think our understanding of God and his Word, and be respectful of each other's opinions. In other words, humility allows us to be open to constructive criticism and creative problem-solving to reconsider how we build our church families.

- We can learn to gracefully listen to one another's stories. This means being willing to sit down and discuss things, *without* imposing our own agendas. It involves sharing how we have sustained wounds, appreciating how those experiences have impacted our lives and faith, then allowing those experiences to inform how we go about doing community life better.
- To be able to help people who have suffered any kind of hurt, it would be useful to be more informed as to how to help, more trauma aware. Training in this area could be valuable, especially in relation to rebuilding trust and providing places that will promote safety and healing.

Religious communities have terrible potential to be *unsafe* places for marginalised people. In recent years, I have begun to appreciate how BRAVE wounded people need to be to step back into community. They dare to believe that there is still something worthwhile in the faith community that invites them to re-enter that potentially harmful space. I honour anyone who has chosen to risk trying again. Thank you. Your courage deserves recognition and a medal of valour. For those of us welcoming these valiant humans into our communities, we need to honour their bravery and earn back their trust. Broken trust is not easily, nor quickly, restored. It takes consistent, persistent love in action over a long time to graciously allow those who have been hurt to trust us (and God) again.

- Whilst those who have been wounded need loving support, our leaders require accountability. There must be transparency and honesty in how we lead these treasured people. Having leaders who are invested in serving their communities, rather than being self-serving, ego-driven, or power-hungry, fosters an environment for good governance and facilitates safe spaces that allow people to heal and flourish.
- We can examine our doctrine and the way we present it. Our understanding of God is an ever-evolving process. We never stop learning. As we re-think our thinking through the lens of love, we can evaluate how our teaching aligns with Jesus' example. In creating inclusive communities, we can appreciate that people will be at different stages of deconstructing and reconstructing their thoughts about God on a whole range of topics. To allow them to flourish, we need to accept people wherever they're at, not expect that they're going to arrive at a certain conclusion at any particular time, and give them the grace to decide how to live in community in ways that are best for them, whilst respecting its values and members.

When I separated from my husband, I became disillusioned with faith and withdrew from my church community. I was dealing with my own heartache and shame, along with the wounds inflicted by the metaphorical wedding planners in my world who tried to pin their expectations and interpretations of scripture on me. I'd almost given up on church. It was only by the grace of God that the very week I had chosen not to return to my church a friend of mine mentioned that he was attending a Catholic church and I asked if I could tag along. I'm so glad he said yes. In that season, I sat towards the back, in a place of complete anonymity. No one could judge or criticise my life choices. I didn't need that. I needed God. I needed healing. I desperately needed somewhere I could nurse my pain and allow myself to be wrapped in Jesus' blanket of love. For six months I sat there. I sat until the Holy Spirit stirred in me a desire to pick myself up and gently begin to give again. In looking for ways to serve my local community, I found a food service for less fortunate people where I offered my help, which led me to the church community to which I now belong. When I arrived at Hamilton Baptist Church, I was still in a very heartbroken state, but they lovingly accepted me where I was at, listened to my story with grace, embraced me on my journey and, in my displacement, gave me somewhere to call home. All of that took time. To them, I am overwhelmingly grateful.

One of the creative challenges we have when re-thinking about thinking about creating flourishing, faith-filled communities, is contemplating the possibilities of how church can be done differently. It doesn't have to look like a traditional church, meeting in traditional buildings. I think most evangelical churches would agree with that. But do we think beyond home churches and Bible Study groups? Do we consider book clubs church? Do we consider just getting together for coffee with a friend church? What about online chat groups? (Whether we talk about theology or not.) Is an interest group like a movie-goers group, gardening collective, running team, kayaking crew, music band… *church*? Can there be church in workplaces, prisons, educational facilities, ships that sail the world…? How do we define church?

Intentionally getting together as a Christian family to focus on knowing Jesus better, worshipping him, and collectively sharing our faith in meaningful ways can be a very significant part of our expression of faith. We usually call those gatherings 'church services'. I am in no way dismissing their importance. As one who has spent over four decades planning and implementing creative church services I can say that I ardently believe in the transformative power and significance of those gatherings. They have been a vital part of my faith journey and I am grateful to all those with whom I've had the privilege of serving alongside. Church services are designed to encourage congregations in their day to day walk with Jesus and equip them to love people throughout their week. Yet the concept of church is far wider than the traditional, weekly service.

> **WE are church. PEOPLE are church. Wherever we are, whomever we're with, we're BEING church.**

The question, then, comes back to LOVE. Are we **being love** to whomever we're with? If so, what is the most loving way to help *this person*, or *these people* to know who Jesus is? How can we meet people where they're at, to love them in that place, and help them know the goodness of God and the beauty of Jesus in their current circumstances? What spaces are we creating that will engage them and give them a sense of belonging, whilst **giving them the freedom to be *who they are*, at *any stage* of their journey**?

One way to re-think how we engage with the idea of church is that **rather than facilitating spaces that people *come to,* we are enabling spaces where people *can be.*** In recent years, as I've undergone my own process of re-thinking about thinking in how we can be the church, one of the values that has become prominent is that of freedom, and how freedom can be fostered in respectful ways that allow people to be themselves at whatever stage of life, and also allow them to give and contribute as they would like.

In graciously enabling these spaces, we offer people freedom from demands, guilt, or judgement. Here are some questions we could possibly be asking where people could find freedom to 'be' church alongside each other: Are we gracious about church attendance or do we frown on those who haven't shown up? Do we create a culture where it's ok to get up and move around in church events so that people can self-regulate if they need to? Are people free to sit or stand, raise their hands or kneel, sing the words, change the words, or stay silent during music worship times? Are people given the freedom to participate and serve with the capacity they have? What pressure are we placing on people to give financially and how can we go about asking for contributions inviting participation without imposing any sense of guilt for those who can't afford to, or don't want to, contribute? What expectations are we placing on people, or is who they are and what they offer simply enough? Are we open to discussion about topics being presented in church teaching and how do we constructively facilitate those discussions? How is the leadership of the church modelling freedom?... I'm sure you could come up with plenty of others.

Cultivating safe spaces that promote healing is one of the greatest challenges we must wrestle with in leading our faith-filled communities. We want people to know Jesus and grow in their understanding of who he is, appreciating how his goodness can infuse their lives. We want people to know that the gospel is still GOOD NEWS! This can be incredibly difficult if someone is hurting from wounds sustained in a faith-based context. Yet, we want to hold on to the fact that Jesus never gives up on us. There IS healing available. Jesus invites us to partner with him in enabling spaces where people can inevitably heal because those spaces are infused with the love of God.

I pray that we can be agents of Jesus' love to one another, as we offer each other his woven blankets of healing.

# Part 6

# FLOURISHING COMMUNITIES WOVEN IN LOVE

# THE BRIDEGROOM'S WOVEN BLANKET
*Scene 6*

Living in a muddy world brought the best, and the worst, out of people. They faced so many challenges that sometimes the complexity of the issues and the enormity of the task seemed overwhelming. How could they possibly find solutions in such a hopelessly muddy world? The murkiness impaired their judgement and decision-making, preventing solutions from ever being perfect. They had to learn to gracefully live with imperfection.

To assist with divisions and disputes, the bridegroom invited his guests to have facilitated discussions to collaboratively solve them, as best they could. It was never seamless, but that wasn't their primary objective. Finding compromises that helped *everyone* was. You see, when the bridegroom assisted these conversations, people began to look beyond their own interests to see what others might be needing and finding resolutions that would help *everyone* flourish.

The bridegroom shared his vision with his guests. He could see beyond the expansive wasteland of mud to all the possibilities that could be gained by working together *in* it. He could see how people could, in fact, *thrive* if they worked together. His vision was one of unity, seeing all his guests loving him and loving one another, whilst caring for themselves. He could see potential for connections to be made, even in the middle of disputes. He could envisage possibilities for people to grow in their unique skills, because they were invited to serve the common good. His perspective was so compelling that guests rallied around his call and dedicated their lives to making their world a better place.

Over time, some guests became builders and support workers. Some became weavers, teachers, and healers. There were visionaries who took a big picture view of the whole situation and administrators who worked out the fine details. Each person found his, her, or their place to help one another in the mud. They committed themselves to the task, and to build unity in the process.

The bridegroom helped too, not only by giving them the tools and resources they needed, but he also set up a school to teach weaving, including how to teach weaving to others. Guests became students. He showed them how to weave intricate, personalised patterns and symbols into their blankets, making them even more beautiful.

As the guests practised wearing and weaving their blankets, they discovered joy in the process. They experienced moments of happiness when they could see people succeeding because of their contributions. Those moments made the whole process worthwhile because they knew – in their deepest heart of hearts – that love was the most beautiful choice, with the most transformational power, they could possibly make. To see someone's life transformed and improved because of the precious gift of love they offered, made all the effort totally worth it. One hundred percent.

So, they continued to work together through the mud with faith, hope, and love.

Their greatest hope was knowing they would one day enjoy the ultimate celebration with the bridegroom. On that day, ALL the mud would be gone. GONE! They would no longer have to struggle, strive, or be burdened by having to wade through it. There would be brand new, pristine wedding outfits for everyone. The old would be gone. The new would come. There would be no more pain or tears, no more divisions or obstacles, no more broken hearts, or fractured relationships. All would be restored. A new world would be formed filled with healing, restoration, and goodness, flooded with the bridegroom's abundant, endless, perfect love.

When that time comes, the mud will disappear
and be replaced with lush, green grass – FOREVER.

***What a glorious day that will be!***

## Chapter 16

# COMMUNITIES WOVEN IN LOVE

Jesus, our master weaver, our loving partner, our bridegroom - the one who is worthy of all praise and honour, glory, and power - lived as one of us to fulfil God's plan for the world and teach us how to weave a life of faith, expressing itself through love.

What a magnificently designed plan it is. From the beginning in Genesis where God offered humanity a whole world to populate, care for and enjoy, to the coming of Jesus whose death and resurrection were pivotal events that represent the restoration of our partnership with God and offer us a new life within a loving community of God's people, which we can celebrate for all the ages to come. No wonder the apostle Paul wrote that no one could possibly imagine what God has planned. (1 Corinthians 2:9) It's mind-blowing!

We find ourselves in our respective cultures and communities, invited to share in Jesus' mandate to go into all the world and make disciples. It is a mandate to love and show others how to love, allowing those effects of love to ripple out and transform the world. His invitation is to build a community of imperfect people who are wholeheartedly devoted to following Jesus with commitment, communion, and celebration. These themes, which we derived from the concept of weddings, are some of the threads we weave on the loom of our lives, scaffolded by the gospel of Jesus' life and ministry, and his death and resurrection.

Let's take a closer look at them one last time as we explore what this looks like as we partner with Jesus in creating restorative communities.

## COMMITMENT:

> **Hebrews 10:24-25:** "Let us consider how we may spur one another to love and good deeds, not giving up meeting together, as some are in the habit of doing, but encouraging one another – and all the more as you see the Day approaching."

Jesus is unquestionably committed to us. His faithfulness is unwavering. (2 Timothy 2:13) Whilst we can look at his example idyllically, we know that in our muddy world we will never live up to that standard of trustworthiness. We break trust with one another all the time. Every time we do something unkind or unloving, or say something misleading or deceitful. Each moment we lash out hurtfully in anger or secretly envy with greed. Whenever we take something that isn't rightfully ours or spread gossip behind someone's back…

It takes commitment to be able to maintain healthy relationships working together in the mud. Being able to stick it out when things get tough isn't easy. This is why grace and forgiveness are so significant. The value we place on the relationships we have is the key to maintaining restorative communities. We have to love each other enough to have honest conversations and stay committed to one another *as* we make messes. (See Chapter 17.)

One of the tensions when valuing individual freedom in a community is how to graciously encourage commitment. How do we balance being committed to one another and having the freedom to choose when, where, and how we express that commitment?

Love doesn't demand, force, coerce, manipulate, or judge. Love patiently waits, kindly invites, humbly accepts, graciously hopes, and lovingly embraces. Isn't that inviting? Isn't a loving community something that people could willingly choose to belong to and participate in? Wouldn't it be exciting that, instead of someone obligatorily saying they have to or are expected to go to church, that they *want* to, *love* to, *can't wait* to, *get* to?

Many of us of my vintage (50+) grew up in an era where church attendance was essentially compulsory. When I was little, I kicked up a fuss one Sunday morning about going to church and asked my father why I had to go. The answer was simple. "Because you have to. It's what we do." There were no further discussions entered into. Fortunately, the lure of cordial and biscuits for morning tea were sufficient incentive to keep me happy. Whilst I'm grateful that my parents instilled the habit of regular church service attendance and the love for Jesus that cultivated in me, now, however, that answer isn't enough, and I've grown to dislike cordial. These days, I want to attend because I LOVE being there.

I love my church family. They're awesome! I can't wait to turn up. It gives me absolute delight to share my Christian journey with others who share the same values, centred around Jesus. I get to help build them up and they build me up too. We learn from each other and do life together. I see it as a privilege to offer my gifts and abilities because I know they will be accepted and appreciated. I have absolute certainty that who I am and whatever I offer is enough.

There are lots of great benefits in meeting regularly – in whatever form that takes. These benefits include things such as providing a sense of belonging, praying for one another, practical help, mutual support, engaging in social events, serving the local and wider community, deepening our relationships, exploring faith, discovering Jesus…

Yes, the benefits are awesome, yet I feel it is more important to understand our 'why'. Why do we 'be' church together? Is it more than a disciplined, 'because the Bible says so' response? I certainly believe so. Assembling as a church family is an expression of love. Love creates unity. Unity is a quality of God that can't be expressed in isolation. Unity is Jesus' ultimate goal for us. This is what he prayed the night before he died:

> **John 17:20-23:** "My prayer is not for them alone. I pray also for those who will believe in me through their message, that all of them may be one, Father, just as you are in me and I am in you. May they also be in us so that the world may believe that you have sent me. I have given them the glory that you gave me, that they may be one as we are one — I in them and you in me — so that they may be brought to complete unity. Then the world will know that you sent me and have loved them even as you have loved me."

**Unity is our 'why'.**

Reconnecting our relationships with restorative love is the solution to the inevitable divisions that will continue to arise amongst us as we live in a muddy world with broken trust. Each time we act in love we are building unity. Building unity creates community.

## COMMUNION:

> **Galatians 3:28:** "There is neither Jew nor Gentile, neither slave nor free, nor is there male and female, for you are all one in Christ Jesus."

Unity is all about being one with each other. But what does that mean? I think this verse sums it up beautifully:

> **Philippians 2:1-4:** "Therefore if you have any encouragement from being united with Christ, if any comfort from his love, if any common sharing in the Spirit, if any tenderness and compassion, then make my joy complete by being like-minded, having the same love, being one in spirit and of one mind. Do nothing out of selfish ambition or vain conceit. Rather, in humility value others above yourselves, not looking to your own interests but each of you to the interests of the others."

**Unity: having the same love, being like-minded, being one in spirit and purpose. We have a similar heart, set of values, and missional purpose, led by the Spirit of God.**

This verse written by the apostle Paul goes on to describe Jesus' character of humility leading him to offer his life for us as a demonstration of love on the cross. Jesus chose to be the means of reconciliation of humanity to God when no one else could. Because of this, he is the one we love, commit to, and partner with, as a bride chooses to partner with her husband.

Our mission as a church is to represent Jesus, be a witness for him, and invite others to know Jesus for themselves through the way we love. As people come to know Jesus, they may wish to be part of our community so that they can be encouraged, motivated, and supported to live in a loving partnership with him.

When we gather as a church, we are focused on Jesus. He is the centre. It is his love that we share. It is his life that we model from. It is his teaching that we try to interpret and apply. From this, we create communities that form their own, unique expressions of love. We weave patterns and symbols into the fabric of our congregations. In my church, there are many threads associated with running analogies because one of our pastors is an avid runner! We thread together traditions and customs. These manifestations of grace are expressions of our common values.

The common values that my church embraces are:

1. We are Jesus focused.
2. We are committed to love.
3. We are diverse and inclusive.
4. We are gracefully present.

Everyone who comes to our church and calls it home identifies with, and embraces, these core values. Your church may have different values. That's ok. There are lots of different kinds of churches, expressing love in lots of different ways. Usually, people gather and form stronger bonds when they have clear, communal values. Collaboration between churches follows the same principle. The centrality of Christianity, however, will always be the person of Jesus. He is the one we partner with now, and will devotedly love for all eternity.

The problem with trying to build unity whilst still living in a muddy world is that it is really hard. We are imperfect people with different ideas, understandings, and interpretations of the Bible, different life experiences, cultures, genders, ages, socio-economic mixes, physical and mental capacities… you get the idea. Yet we come together to celebrate Jesus and use the gifts and abilities we have to serve one another, empowered and led by the Holy Spirit, with a heart of loving humility.

Despite our good intentions, we still get it wrong. We still manage to hurt one another and come into conflict with each other. Let's be real. We're never going to do this perfectly while we live this side of heaven. The new order hasn't come yet, so we have to learn to live with one another in an imperfect, muddy world. This is why Jesus spent so much time teaching his disciples how to love. He taught concepts of grace, mercy, forgiveness, acceptance, overlooking offences, not judging one another, learning to settle disputes and handle conflicts, offering healing, and showing kindness – even when it doesn't seem deserved.

Embracing Jesus and embodying kingdom values are what set us apart as Christian communities of faith. How we handle all the struggles, mistakes, failures, and challenges of living in community is what defines us. In the end, the main question that will be asked of us is: How well did we love the people we have come in contact with throughout our lives? Have we offered them a woven blanket of love?

**CELEBRATION:**

Coming together as a diverse body of believers and managing to do anything collaboratively is a miracle in itself. In that sense, the life Jesus invites us to is downright miraculous. It is SO worth celebrating! In over fifty years of Christian living I've discovered the joy and delight of celebrating with my church family. When I have good news, I want to share it with them. When I'm going through difficult times, I ask them for prayer and support. The highs and lows, the joys and tears, the excitement and disillusionment, the embraces and the conflict… The mixture of all the mud with all the beauty… THAT is the abundant life Jesus invites us to.

> **John 10:10:** "I have come that they may have life, and have it to the full." *(Abbreviated)*

An abundant life isn't one devoid of sin, pain, hurt, disappointment, frustration, or challenges. An abundant life is one empowered by the Spirit of God to face all of life's hardships whilst living in a loving partnership with Jesus. (John 16:33, Romans 8:31-39)

> **Jesus teaches us to weave love through the harshest of conditions, the most painful of circumstances with the most challenging of people.**
> ***That* is the miracle and wonder of love.**

One of the ways that we are empowered in our Christian walk is through practising spiritual disciplines. Jesus' response about him being a bridegroom was related to a question about fasting. Fasting, prayer, reading the Bible, studying it, meditating on it, memorising scripture, attending church services, are all activities that we can do to enhance our relationship with Jesus.

One of the controversies of commitment versus freedom is, again, the tension of doing things motivated by love rather than obligation. I believe in freedom (which means I don't *have* to do any of those things to be in a relationship with Jesus), but I also know how practising spiritual disciplines has strengthened and shaped my faith, and allowed God to transform and empower me. I'd encourage you not to throw them out for the sake of spiritual liberation, but cultivate them in whichever ways help you, for the current season of your life, to keep growing in your relationship with Jesus.

One of the most significant benefits to practising spiritual disciplines is that they help align our hearts with God's. These simple practices open our hearts to Jesus, and allow the Holy Spirit to form his character and values in us. Like with any relationship, the more time we spend with someone, the more their attitudes and mannerisms rub off on us. How much more when we spend time with Jesus? He can help us become more graciously loving, compassionate, understanding, helpful, kind, patient… The list could go on, and on, and ON!

God's invitation to us is to be in relationship with him. That begins here and now, empowering us to live our faith by expressing it in simple acts of love in everyday life. That is our new mandate as his people. My prayer is that our witness as the church of Jesus would be welcoming and attractive, where people feel free to express their love for Jesus and his people in the ways the Holy Spirit directs them, as unique expressions of their true, authentic selves. And where people feel like they can unreservedly belong and call their church community 'home'.

## Chapter 17
# TRUTH WOVEN IN LOVE

Discipleship is all about coming alongside one another and offering Jesus' blanket of love; learning to weave new threads, patterns, and symbols into our unique coverings that represent our relationship with him. This is how we build community. This is how we express love.

Coming alongside one another presents a huge challenge: we are all different. We think differently, work differently, and live differently. Embracing the diversity of our differences is one of the most glorious expressions of Christian community. It is also the hardest. It raises questions of all kinds, like how do we build community? How do we express our faith? How do we worship God? How do we share our appreciation of Jesus with the world? How do we collaborate with one another? How do we lovingly embrace and accept one another? How can we be gracefully present with each other? For every question asked there are as many answers as there are people in the church - and outside the church, for that matter!

How? Why? Who? What? When? Where? So many questions! Too many to list, and yet faced by everyone. Yes, this isn't an issue reserved for

Christians. It is the challenge of the *world*. How do we get along with one another and create safe spaces of healthy, productive living in our homes, workplaces, sporting clubs, political arenas, military bases, construction sites, emergency services, farms, schools, hospitals… even the international space station? Name the communal space and you'll find the communal dilemma.

I believe the answer lies in our ability to have healthy, open, honest conversations; conversations seasoned with God's grace. (Colossians 4:6) This, in itself, is a huge topic so I will offer a condensed perspective.

One of the greatest challenges to living a life of faith, expressed in love, is seeing those around us making life choices that seem to be out of line with God's character or values, according to our worldview and interpretation of scripture. In other words, using their freedom to make choices with destructive consequences. There is precedent in the Bible of lovingly coming alongside one another and offering caring advice to gently restore and lovingly correct behaviour. (Matthew 18:15-20, Galatians 6:1-2) In Ephesians, Paul recommends that we 'speak the truth in love'. (Ephesians 4:15)

> Using the metaphor of this book,
> I've called it '*weaving* the truth in love.'

Discipleship is about teaching and encouraging others to assess their actions in the light of God's love. His Word illuminates where we struggle to offer genuine love, exhibit behaviour that is unhelpful to ourselves or others, or have motives that aren't honourable. Yet, our own perceptions are coloured, even distorted, by our experiences. We can't claim to know the whole truth (1 Corinthians 13:9), nor can we judge from a position of spiritual elitism because we are all covered in the same mud. We need the empowering of the Holy Spirit to lead us into the truth of a matter, and not simply assume that we know it all. (John 16:13).

Therein lies the tension: To speak or not to speak. As disciples, we are called to weave the truth in love, especially in relation to accountability with our leaders. There is a place for correction and addressing sin, but it needs to be done motivated by, and in the context of, love. It needs to be a cooperative process, not a confrontational one.

To not lovingly attempt to correct someone when they are hurting themselves or others is doing them a disservice. It would be unloving of us not to intervene, but not with a pointed, judgemental finger, nor superiority of 'purity' or 'knowledge of God'. This attitude is harmful.

A loving way of addressing this is by asking, **"How are we empowering people to autonomously make good, wise, healthy choices, and how do those choices impact God, themselves, others, and their communities?"**

What follows are some recommendations of how to gracefully, lovingly, and gently have conversations that build relationships with others who are struggling with their mud, whilst recognising that we, too, are wading through the same swamp. I tread carefully and ask you to sift through these suggestions and take what is helpful to you. (1 Thessalonians 5:19-22)

- We can consider if we are the best person or if there's someone more suited to have this conversation, and if this an appropriate time to intervene.
- If we are the right person at the right time, we then need to examine our own hearts, before addressing someone elses'. We have to admit that we are all in the same situation, wading through mud. We must address the sin in our own lives first, so that we can talk with someone openly without judgement or criticism, with humility and deep care for their wellbeing, and not just frustrated by

someone's annoying habits or mannerisms. (Matthew 7:3-5) It is possible that our need to step in may have vanished after dealing with our own heart first. To do this, we need to examine behaviour (both ours and others) in line with scripture. This is where mud gets even muckier because we each have our own interpretation of scripture. Let's look to Jesus for guidance. Rather than taking a legalistic approach, Jesus taught his disciples how to see things through the eyes of love. He healed on the Sabbath. He ate with sinners. He spoke with social rejects. (Shock! Horror!) He practised loving freedom.

**Jesus went against the 'rules' of religious expectation and showed that love trumps all laws.**

We can ask the same question of both ourselves and of others: Is the behaviour loving towards God, one's self, others, and the community? Does it align with the character of God and the values of his kingdom? If not, then a loving conversation may be helpful in directing someone to find more beneficial ways of behaving. In addition, we offer care, support, grace, acceptance, forgiveness, and the wisdom of the Holy Spirit wrapped in a blanket of his all-encompassing love.

- One of the most valuable things we can do is to affirm our relationship, appreciating what that person contributes to our lives. This sets a tone for a conversation based on gratitude and inspires confidence that the intent of whatever is discussed will continue building and strengthening our relationship, rather than being destructive and harmful. Disingenuousness or insincerity are quickly seen through.

- Being able to wrap someone in a blanket of love can only come from trust and respect. Then we can find out a person's story, from their perspective, based on their life experience. Once we understand their story, we can begin to ask deeper questions about their behaviour and look into the heart of the matter. This approach invites collaboration, asking them what *they* think, what *they* could do, what choices *they* could make. It's all about graciously serving THEM. We can't just view someone's actions and think that by changing their behaviour we're going to change them as a person. It doesn't work like that. For any behaviour we have, there is a belief system that it is embedded in with a foundation of values that it has been established by, usually formed growing up by deeply impactful, emotional experiences. That's not something to take lightly, nor will it be healed through a 'one-method-fits-all' approach. We need the wisdom and insight of the Holy Spirit to work out how to support others and walk alongside them, treating each situation case by case. This includes knowing when to refer someone to an expert with more specialist knowledge, like a counsellor, psychologist, or support worker.
- Part of effective communication is the ability to practise active listening skills. Maybe we could find out more about them. What is the Holy Spirit doing *in* them? How can we encourage them in their partnership with God? We can listen with empathy, care, and genuine curiosity, wanting to get to know the person. We need to be careful about imposing our own biases and assumptions. Perhaps their behaviour is something we don't *like*, rather than inherently against God's values.
- A gentle approach to dealing with a tricky issue is by treating it like sitting side-by-side, working on a jigsaw puzzle together, putting

all the pieces on a table, and looking at them from different perspectives, then cooperatively solving the issues. This way, the *issues* are the problem, not the person. This is a constructive way to work things out together and be creative problem-solvers, rather than confrontational attackers.

- It's only after someone has their 'why' (what is at their heart's core), that they can begin to re-think about thinking (repent) so that those deep-seated beliefs can change. This can require profound, inner healing, and can potentially take a long time. We need to be patient enough to bear each other's burdens in our messy state (Galatians 6:2) and accept that we are each doing the best that we can with the resources we have at any given time. Re-thinking is a process of transformation, which is the work of the Holy Spirit. (2 Corinthians 3:18) By faith, we trust that he will work in us, and in those around us, in his time, in his order, with his methods. Our job is to partner with him in what *he* is doing, not what we think should be done. If we are genuinely concerned about someone, then we need to be willing to walk with them through this process. This shows our loving commitment to them - just as they are, wherever they're at. This is a significant way in which we build community.
- Being practical, there are some important things to consider when preparing to have a meaningful conversation.

**The TIMING:** It's important to find a mutually suitable time to have these conversations. Allow enough time. A rushed conversation with time pressure won't facilitate a relaxed, open conversation.

**The WHERE:** Think through the venue. Having a heart to heart at the school gate at pick up time would be a disaster!

Consider seating arrangements and help everyone feel at ease and supported, as much as possible. This includes being aware of any power imbalances that may be present, like having a home team advantage. Finding a neutral place is preferable.

**The HOW:** How a meeting is conducted can be the make or break of a relationship. This includes the tone of the conversation, whether the person feels welcome and safe. Safety is all about trust. The idea is to help anyone who is being spoken with feel like they are not being judged, that they are not on trial, that there is space for open, honest conversation that is going to lead them to a better place and a healthier relationship. If they feel attacked, accused, abused, or unheard they will not respond, and even greater damage will be done. *How* we do things matters. What are our priorities? Getting the result we want or valuing, respecting, and caring for the other person/people in the process? What is the *real* goal of the conversation?

- We can pray for the Holy Spirit's empowerment to lovingly care for one another. We can ask for wisdom to guard our own hearts and practise self-care whilst we care for others. We can ask for discernment about putting in place appropriate boundaries with people. We can practise the loving act of offering someone the freedom to be themselves and walk with God in their own way, at their own pace and develop their own understanding of who he is and how his life can find expression in theirs.
- Finally, we need to appreciate that not everyone will accept our help, support, and advice. Some people won't want to change. For others, it may not be the right timing to receive instruction. When we meet resistance, we need to graciously allow God to work in

their lives as that person chooses to partner with him, or not! Then entrust them to his loving care. Trying to impose our ideals or force someone to change when they're not ready can only lead to harm. We need God's wisdom to know when to hold on, and when to let go. (Ecclesiastes 3:1-11)

Does that sound gracious to you? Does offering someone advice and allowing them to sift through your words and apply them in their own way that is helpful and resourceful to them feel freeing? It is! That's how Jesus taught.

Having open, honest conversations is one of the most challenging, yet potentially life-impacting things we can do in building community with one another. This allows us to be honest about how we feel and maintain our authenticity, whilst creating opportunities to build stronger connections with each other. If we are open to correction and have a teachable heart, then those conversations can help change the direction of our lives to become more loving, fulfilling, and abundant. We can help point people to Jesus, the source of all our help and hope, knowing that he is far more passionate and committed to his church than we could ever hope to be. In him are all the resources that we will need to keep living this life of faith, expressing itself in love. (2 Corinthians 9:8)

# Chapter 18

# UNITED IN CHRIST, CONNECTED WITH EACH OTHER

Repent and believe. Two key words.

The ability to re-think our thinking and align our hearts to God's is the essence of the life-long process of discipleship. What we believe determines our thoughts, our decisions, and consequently our actions. Every single decision we make has a ripple effect. Are those decisions going to help us and our world flourish, or not? The answer isn't clear-cut, straightforward, or easy-going. It's arduous, messy, and fraught with relational complexities. Therein lies the question: If it's so hard, why bother caring?

I'll share with you a glimpse of the lowest point in my life. In my season of separation, after one particularly heartbreaking family event, I found myself holding back my tears, escaping the function hall, and speeding off into the night. No direction. No seatbelt. No thought of consideration to myself.

I found myself driving up to a lookout and reached the top. As I looked out over the city, the emotional dam burst and I wept uncontrollably. I desperately grieved the loss of my family and felt like I no longer belonged with them. I also recognised that the way my extended family were treating me was an expression of the pain they were experiencing in response to my choice to divorce my husband. My thoughts took me down a dark road. If my decision to separate was going to hurt the people I'd loved the most, then what was the point in me still being around? Maybe they were better off without me. I loved them more than anything else in my world and now that world had imploded. What did I have left? My heart was numb. My life felt empty. I lost the will to care.

That night, and for some time after, I simply didn't care what happened to me. I didn't go out of my way to self-harm, but I did little to protect myself either. I felt like my life didn't matter. I existed in a zombie-like state of detached, emotional indifference. Fortunately, I had some loving, close friends who told me, in no uncertain terms, that I did, in fact, matter. My life mattered. And I mattered to God.

Maybe this is something that you, also, need to hear: YOU MATTER. You are an incredibly precious person who is dearly loved by God. You are worthy to be loved, valued, recognised, and appreciated. No matter who you are, what you've done, or what you've lived through, his love for you is infinite and forever faithful.

You see, the good news of Jesus is that we matter. We are the most precious beings in the entire universe to him. Our choices also matter, along with their consequences. He cares about ALL of it and ALL of us. His Holy Spirit can give us the heart to care too.

For starters, God gently reminded me that I needed to care about myself and that even through my most agonising heartaches he was still with me. He widened my outlook and reminded me that my life still had purpose.

He also showed me how my indifference could potentially hurt the people around me, even more than the separation. Something as simple as choosing to wear a seatbelt when driving can make a difference. I just had to choose to care enough how my actions could impact others to make a small change in my driving behaviour.

Sometimes, we stop caring because we don't believe in our own worth. Other times, we stop caring because we put our own interests above the interests of others. Being self-focused is an easier way to live. It's also very culturally acceptable, especially in this era where individualism and consumerism are so unrestrained.

Yet, Jesus invites us into a counter-cultural way of thinking. He invites us to follow his law of love: freedom WITH the responsibility of considering how our choices impact the lives of others. If we can re-think our thinking (repent) and come to accept that this is the best way to live (believe) then we are living lives of faith, which inevitably express themselves in loving actions towards ourselves, others, our world, and ultimately God.

On the other hand, to not trust that this is the best way to live is what God defines as sin. In this light, sin is thoughtless indifference. It is simply not caring. But that's exactly why we have the Holy Spirit, who changes our thoughts and opens our hearts to begin to care, despite the complications that caring brings.

As we've discovered, repentance is more than a moment of guilt and saying sorry. It is even more than a mindset of teachable humility. It is a deeply formed heart-set that allows our spirits to be moulded into the image of Jesus, reflecting his character, and living in his ways. This beautiful disposition changes what we believe, which informs our choices and directs our lives. It allows us to be open to the possibility of seeing new perspectives and new opportunities. It also empowers us to change from our old ways of living to embrace a freer, more loving approach. Rather than being legalistic and rule-driven in how we implement scripture, we learn to live according to the value of love, the overarching law that covers everything.

Through repentance we can begin to imagine fresh vision for our lives and for the church. We can dare to hope that things CAN get better, relationships CAN be restored, and life CAN be resurrected – just as Jesus demonstrated.

For me, I live in much brighter times now. I love the evolving relationships I have with my two children, and I have done so much re-thinking about life that I can truly say that I am a different person to who I was a decade ago. I have a new life in Christ. I am thankful for God's grace, forgiveness, and unfailing love which have held me through so many challenges and continue to shape me into the person he already knows I will be in the future.

Through all our re-thinking about thinking I hope that you have begun to believe that knowing Jesus and having a relationship with him is good news. It really is! His teaching is relevant and life-giving, intending us to flourish as individuals and collectively as his family. Being an apprentice of the way Jesus demonstrated love is both a challenge and an inspiration. His law of love sparks so many questions and issues for discussion that it will take a lifetime of discovery to even begin to scratch the surface of how to implement it. Perhaps that's why we have an eternity to practise.

For now, our purpose is to work together in our muddy conditions to find creative, constructive, and authentic ways to love each other, whilst forming our own relationship with Jesus and caring for ourselves in the process. This is how we live out his law of love with loving freedom.

If I had to summarise this book, the purpose of Christianity, the message of Jesus, and the heartbeat of discipleship in one simple phrase it would be:

**'United in Christ, connected with each other.'**

The purpose of love is unity. Love unites us with Jesus. Jesus' work on the cross facilitated our unity with him, and his resurrection secured it forever. His love also invites us into his ministry of reconciliation with one another, building bridges of connection which unite us. (2 Corinthians 5:18-21) We cannot have unity with one another unless we care about each other. For this, we have the Holy Spirit's help. He is the essence of love in spirit form who empowers us to live in love.

Jesus helps us weave thoughtful expressions of kindness into the fabric of our lives as we learn to offer who we are and what we have – in the middle of the muckiness of life – to serve one another. The ripple effects of love have the potential not only to encompass the globe, but to also overflow to future generations, leaving a legacy throughout history.

As we grow in our faith and find healing for our hearts, we may find ourselves drawn to help others who are hurt or suffering. We may respond to social justice issues and want to right the wrongs in our societies. We may also find ways of lovingly caring for this magnificent planet. As a family of God, there is enormous power in collaborating towards making this world a better place. Jesus loves justice. His heart breaks for the marginalised, destitute, and rejected. He invites us to partner with him to love and embrace them, empowering them to thrive and find a place where they can belong.

One of the challenges we have in exercising loving freedom is respecting that we will all bring our unique expressions to responding to the world's needs. Some people will care more about some issues than others. We will also disagree on methodologies and use of resources. We will inevitably find ourselves in conflict. We will get things wrong. We will make mistakes. We will create mucky messes.

This means we must keep pointing people to Jesus and relying on him to help us maintain our unity, despite our differences. After all, he is the ultimate teacher! We can practise recognising when we've hurt someone, offering an apology, asking for forgiveness, and showing how we have changed and want to do things differently. We can also create safe spaces where people can heal. These spaces are welcoming, inclusive, accepting, gracious, empowering, collaborative, and respectful. They require good governance that is transparent and accountable, where issues can be addressed appropriately so that safety is maintained. Doing this engenders trust. Trust fosters unity.

The good news of the gospel is that no matter how much mess we've made, nothing is beyond the transformational power of Jesus' love. We may have to work through the complexities of the consequences of our choices, but his hope can breathe new life into the hardest of hearts and bring light into the darkest of circumstances. The way we do this is by weaving the truth with love, speaking graciously to one another, and supporting each other as we re-think our actions and try to align our decisions with Jesus' character and values. Healthy choices produce fruitful lives.

Love invites us to listen to one another's stories and offer kindness, free from demands, expectations, or judgement. Love graciously allows people to 'be'. As we learn to 'be', we practise 'being' the church with each other, enabling spaces that allow human beings to flourish. This has the power to shape the narrative of our lives, the collection of our stories that we take with us to share throughout eternity.

What will our stories say about us and how we chose to treat one another?

I hope that this book serves to be fuel for the Holy Spirit to ignite in you a flame of passion for Jesus and his church. I pray that the Holy Spirit will give you the gift of faith (Ephesians 2:8-9) to believe that God's directive of loving freedom is the most fulfilling way to live. I pray his heartbeat of love will resonate in yours as you take his love and freely, generously, and authentically share it with your world. May we ever stay focused on Jesus, our master weaver, as he continues to teach us how to weave this extraordinary life of faith, expressing itself in love.

## CONCLUSION
# DANCING IN THE MUD

The bridegroom's woven blanket is a gift of love that Jesus offers each and every one of us. We can choose to accept it, and if we do, we can choose to put it on and wear it. We can choose to partner with Jesus and keep weaving into it intricate symbols and patterns as we sew a unique life of love with him. We can live by faith, trusting that wearing his blanket makes a difference to how we live and the positive impact that can make on the world.

We can offer others comfort with our blankets and even offer them their own unique blanket if they'd like one. It's up to them to accept it. Not everyone will. Some people will keep struggling and striving through the mud without it because that is all they know. Some people will get hurt in the process of helping others and may take their blankets off, and go their own way. These people give up on the bridegroom and his mission. Maybe that is *you*? The offer of the blanket is still there if you want it. The offer will **always** be there. So is the empowering strength and healing love that comes with it.

For those who choose to embrace their mission and keep trusting the bridegroom in a woven life of partnership, there is rich reward. They get to know the bridegroom more intimately. They cultivate deeper relationships with other people. They discover the beauty of compassion, forgiveness, acceptance, kindness, and inclusion. Grace fills their lives and love governs their steps. They find richness in life and a sense of fulfillment in helping others.

**They learn to dance in the mud.**

You may realise by now, that we are each guests of the bridegroom, like Jesus described in Mark 2. Collectively, we are all part of the picture represented by the bride in Revelation 21. We are all in this together. We all have a role to play. We are all loved and accepted by the bridegroom, and he invites us to help one another through this messy, mucky journey we call life. With him, we are no longer trudging. With him, we are empowered by his Spirit to find joy and strength to weave purposeful lives of love.

The invitation is there for you – like a treasured, gift-wrapped box, to take out the beautifully hand-woven blanket Jesus offers you and to put it on, trusting by faith that ***a life woven in love*** will ultimately be the most beautiful expression of life you could possibly live.

Will you accept it?

I hope you say, "I do."

# A PRAYER

"Our loving God, we thank you that you sent your son Jesus, our bridegroom, to earth.

Jesus, we thank you that you demonstrated how to live a life of faith, expressing itself in love. In becoming a human being and living as one of us, you showed us what commitment is and what it is to share life with you and celebrate it together as your family. We look forward to doing that with you forever. Keep teaching us through your words and example how to love ourselves, each other, and you, wholeheartedly.

Holy Spirit, as we go out into our day, into our week, I pray that we will partner with you in the work that you are doing in the world and that, by weaving our lives together, we will see people's lives and whole communities transformed as we graciously offer them your love.

In Jesus' name, Amen."

# Part 7
# FINAL COMMENTS

# A VISION OF COMMUNITY

A t heart, I am an idealist. I believe in God's Kingdom and I long to see it outworked 'on earth as it is in heaven.' (Matthew 6:10b) In 2007, I began to write an unfolding dream of what heaven on earth could look like. The form of this vision is inspired by Martin Luther King, who dared to dream of a better world for his people. This evolving dream is a picture for the church that reflects the brilliance of Jesus. Yes, it's idealistic and we will never reach perfection on this side of heaven because we wade through the mud of life, but isn't it inspiring to have a vision to look forward to and work towards as we build flourishing communities together?

## **<u>I HAVE A DREAM</u>**

I have a dream where God's church will rise with a passion for Jesus as the world has never seen. Where hearts will be devoted to the adoration of his powerful name. Where people on earth who believe in his name will, as one body, with one voice, and one Lord, Jesus Christ, herald a magnificent song of joy, triumphant in victory, radiant in righteousness, waiting with eager anticipation for the coming of their wonderful King.

I have a dream where people grow in a vibrant partnership with Jesus. Where they discover their identity in him, know their self-worth, appreciate their uniqueness, and protect their hearts. Where they walk in deepest intimacy, worship in sincere devotion, bear fruit with effortless abiding, and live in complete rest.

I have a dream where Jesus' church will be wholeheartedly devoted to prayer. Where she will intercede for the helpless, the hopeless, the rejected, the poor, the destitute, and the forgotten, so they can find refuge and hope in the embodiment of Jesus – the church. Where the expression of her love, the kindness of her heart, the charity of her compassion, and the honesty of her words will draw those in darkness into Christ's glorious light. Where they will find healing and wholeness, freedom and forgiveness, joy and gladness, and contentment and peace as they rest in the arms of their loving saviour.

I have a dream where the church will cry out against injustice. Where she will rescue the ravaged, feed the hungry, befriend the lonely, embrace the marginalised, comfort the grieving, and shelter the weathered. Where she will never be weary of doing what is good, right, and just.

I have a dream of a body of believers where people are treasured. Where the elderly are valued, invalids are supported, orphans are parented, widows are defended, and the disfigured are covered. Where the value and respect of human life are upheld. Where people are welcomed with genuine care and affirmed in their authenticity. Where they are encouraged to explore their faith, develop their gifts, cultivate their passions, grow in wisdom, and walk in integrity. Where diversity is celebrated and inclusion is fostered.

I have a dream where the expression of the church is in heartfelt worship, reverent awe, and vibrant celebration of Jesus. Where praise and thanksgiving are incessant companions to the honouring acts of service by the saints. Where knees bow humbly in deepest gratitude for all his hand has provided and mercifully pray for his Spirit to lead and empower them and establish the work of their hands.

I have a dream where the church will listen and respond to the voice of God's Spirit. Where she will walk in power and authority by his enabling. Where the Holy Spirit will be free to move in healings, wonders, and miracles. Where the signs of God accompany his people as they share his Word with humility, teachability, and kindness. Where scripture is taught graciously, clearly, and respectfully, examined through the lens of love. Where the timeless and universal truth of God brings a timely and relevant message for now.

I have a dream where the church explodes creativity with vitality and excellence. Where every stroke of the brush, every music note played, every step which is danced, every act which is theatred, and every clay that is sculpted honours the glorious name of Jesus. Where each generation rises to sing a new song to the Lord and cries out to every culture, tribe, and nation: "HOPE TO THE WORLD!"

I have a dream where all the gifts of the Spirit are acknowledged and used effectively by believers for the edification of the church and the expansion of the kingdom. Where prophecy is valued and the Spirit's flame is fanned. Where every act is motivated by love.

I have a dream of a great joining in leadership across the world between apostles, teachers, evangelists, prophets, and pastors who work in humility and unity under the anointed power of Jesus' Holy Spirit to lead and equip God's people for service, and to build the church with the life-giving gospel of Christ, centred on his demonstration of extraordinary, unfailing love.

I have a dream where all those in authority in the church lead purposefully with integrity, order, and accountability. Where those who are mature teach those who are young. Where the young are encouraged, equipped, and strengthened and, in turn, inspire those older by their commitment, vigour, and determination.

I have a dream where children grow up knowing who they are in Jesus, walking in the certainty of their calling with vision, hope, and faith, unashamed to be children of God.

I have a dream where all of God's people love the Lord and love one another deeply. Where they share life together in fellowship and food, friendship, and fun. Where Christians laugh and cry together, embrace and uphold one another, and bear each other's burdens. Where they live sacrificially, give generously, speak truthfully, praise joyfully, serve faithfully, pray earnestly, and stand valiantly. Where the church as one body hopes in all things, believes in all things, and trusts in all things that love never fails.

I have a dream where churches are united as ONE under the Lordship of Jesus Christ in spirit, mind, purpose, and passion. Where God's family acts humbly with mercy, works selflessly in harmony, and shares cheerfully in the cause of the gospel. Where grace and forgiveness abound, and where the Holy Spirit perfects God's people making them more and more like Jesus. Where wisdom is sought, Biblical principles are practised, education is provided, healthy living is promoted, counselling is given, conflicts are resolved, peace is pursued, unity is preserved, families are upheld, community is cherished, and where true freedom is lived.

I have a dream where the church will stand and declare to the nations the invincible exaltation that "OUR GOD REIGNS!" Where she will be robed in righteousness through the forgiveness of Jesus by the power of his death and resurrection.

I have a dream of a glorious multitude, flawless in beauty and perfect in holiness, standing before the King of Kings and Lord of Lords. Where a thunderous applause rises from within their hearts to join the whole host of angels in resounding the rapturous anthem "HOLY, HOLY, HOLY IS THE LORD GOD ALMIGHTY. HEAVEN AND EARTH ARE FULL OF YOUR GLORY. HOSANNA IN THE HIGHEST!"

   The bridegroom descends triumphantly.
        His glory shines resplendently.
            He lifts his bride majestically
                to carry her home to eternity.
                                  Amen. Amen. Amen.

# THE BRIDEGROOM'S WOVEN BLANKET

## THE COMPILED STORY

Picture a beautiful bride. It's the day of her wedding. She's dressed in a long, white wedding gown that fits her perfectly. Her hair is done up and not a strand is out of place. She looks resplendent from head to toe. She is absolutely spotless. She's totally gorgeous. She's prepared. She's ready.

The limousine comes to pick her up to take her to the church where her future husband awaits.

"Congratulations, Ma'am," the chauffeur says as he opens the door for her.

"Thank you!" she replies excitedly as she takes her seat.

They set off. The bride can feel butterflies in her tummy as she spots the church in the distance, knowing her future husband is there waiting for her…

Riding comfortably in the limo, the bride smiles to herself, picturing her husband waiting for her at the church.

Unfortunately, the beautiful image she envisioned is suddenly jolted from her mind by the sound of loud splutter ka-thunk of the engine as the limo shudders to a halt, breaking down. Despite the bride's attempt to will the car into motion it refuses to budge any further.

The limo driver turns to the bride and says, "I'm sorry ma'am. You'll have to walk."

He gets out of the car and opens the door for her. She steps out, but her beautiful white shoe lands in a puddle of mud.

The driver highlights her predicament. "Sorry, ma'am," he apologises. "It's like that *all* the way."

The bride looks up from her muddied shoe to view the panorama. As far as she can see there is mud. It's an impossibly big, swamp-like puddle. She realises that she can't go around it. It's too far. There's no helicopter to fly her over it. She's just going to have to walk *through* it.

In her heart, the bride knows there is no other place in the world she wants to be. Her husband and the life she longs to build with him are there, waiting for her; so close, and yet so… far… away. She steps out. She puts her foot boldly into the mud, hoping to clean her shoes when she reaches the other side.

The bride is determined. She starts to walk, yet the more steps she takes she realises that the mud is a LOT deeper and a LOT harder to move through than she expected. At first, the hem of her dress gets dirty. Then she finds that the mud is reaching up to her knees and she's straining to push her way through it. She keeps moving forward. She's *got* to get there. But just when she thinks the worst is over, she falls, headfirst. She tears her dress and is covered in filth.

By the time the bride reaches the steps of the church she's a complete mess…

Unexpectedly, the bride is greeted by a lovely, experienced, neatly dressed wedding planner who says to her, "Oh my! Deary me! You've been through a bit of muck, haven't you?" (For some reason she has a British accent.) "Dry your tears, love. It will be *all* right."

The bride wipes her eyes with her hands but is interrupted by the wedding planner.

"Ohhh! Best not, pet. Now you've got more mud on your face. Shame, that." She clicks her tongue.

"What am I supposed to do?" the bride cries out.

"Don't you worry about a thing, love," the planner consoles. "I've got something here that will make everything *perfect*."

She unzips a little purse buckled around her waist where she keeps all her bits and bobs for bridal emergencies and pulls out a beautiful, hand-sized piece of white, satin fabric.

"Here we are, dear. This will do *just* the trick."

The bride stares at her with a puzzled look.

The wedding planner gets out some pins and fastens the piece of fabric on to the tear on her dress. Then she stands back and admires her work, looking at her little patch of white satin, yet ignoring the fact that the pins are beginning to rip the dress and that blobs of mud are starting to seep through from the dress, staining the little piece of material.

"Ah! My work is done. You can go in now, love. Off you go dear, spit spot."

Zipping up her little purse, the wedding planner departs.

The bride is left on the steps of the church in utter disbelief. The patch of material cannot fix the tear or cover the mud. She doesn't know what to do. Worst still, she's so embarrassed and ashamed of the state of her dress and the muck all over her that she doesn't dare go through the doors of the church to face her husband who is waiting inside. All she can do is fall on the steps, bury her face in her hands, and cry…

The groom heard his bride sobbing. Now, we know that the groom isn't supposed to see the bride before the wedding, but he defied tradition and came out anyway. He picked her up and wiped her tears. He held her in his arms.

She tried to pull away.

The groom sensed her shame and embarrassment and held her reassuringly, lifting her head so she could look in his eyes.

"I love you," he said, "with all my heart. You are more beautiful to me now than you have ever been."

The bride couldn't believe what she was hearing. She didn't feel beautiful. All she felt was terrible shame.

"How can that possibly be?" she asked. "Look at me. I'm covered in mud."

She stepped back so he could see all the muck that covered her.

"My lovely bride," he replied, "when I look at you, I see absolute perfection. I don't see mud. I see your beautiful heart. A heart that devotedly loves me, that would wade through filth to reach me, to be with me – forever."

At that moment, the bride felt he could see right through her, to the core of her being. She felt naked and exposed yet completely loved. He was right. She loved him, more than anything else in the whole world.

The groom took her hands in his, looking at her sparkling engagement ring.

"It's going to be ok. I promise. I knew about the mud. I've got this sorted. I have a wonderful surprise for you: the most gorgeous, sparkling, clean dress is on its way. Trust me. You'll love it and look stunning."

The bride, for the first time, felt a glimmer of hope spread through her, but then she saw her stained dress...

It was like her husband could read her mind.

"Wait here," he said, as he disappeared into the church and brought out a big, white box, tied with a golden ribbon.

"You bought me a *gift?*" the bride asked incredulously, but her husband-to-be just smiled at the love of his life and gave her the box.

Gently and curiously, she took it and untied the ribbon. She lifted the lid and saw the most beautiful hand-woven blanket she had ever seen. She gasped.

"Did you… did you weave this yourself?" She knew he was a craftsman, but never suspected that he knew how to weave, and certainly not this expertly.

He smiled and nodded. "A man of hidden talents," he winked.

"I… I can't believe it. It's incredible."

As she took the blanket out of the box, she discovered intricate patterns and pictures that representing shared memories, blended with colours reflecting each season of the relationship they'd cultivated. There were bright golds and pinks and purples, and darker hues of greys and blues and greens. There were symbolic tear drops and rays of sunshine, images representing special moments that filled their universe. In the centre of it all was a tree. She recognised it instantly. It left her breathless…

"It's our tree," she whispered. "Where we met."

He nodded.

"You and I are amazing together. Think about how much we've been able to do and give already, and our life together has barely begun." He squeezed her hand and kissed her forehead.

"I don't know what to say. How can I thank you?" she asked sincerely.

"Well, put it on!" he exclaimed, wrapping it around her shoulders, covering her beautifully. Despite its rich texture it felt so soft and light, gracing her in a magnificent woven tapestry of story and colour.

The groom thought his heart would burst as she twirled around in the woven blanket.

"You don't need to see the mud anymore, sweetheart. Just look at *this* and remember the beautiful life we are weaving together."

Then he took her in his arms and whispered tenderly, "I am still committed to you. I love you unconditionally. Don't be ashamed or embarrassed. All *I* want is to marry you and celebrate our life together forever. Do you still want that with **me**?"

Wrapped in her glorious, woven blanket, with glistening tears and a beaming smile, the bride held her future husband's hand and spoke words that flowed from the depths of her heart.

"I do."

The bride stood with her future husband at the top of the stairs at the entrance of the church. They held one another tightly, reassuring each other of their beautiful promise of life together. The bride was covered in her woven blanket. The groom didn't see the mud, only her blanket adorned with the colours, symbols, and patterns of the life they were weaving together…

So enraptured were they in that moment, that the bride had failed to notice something significant: the absence of their guests. No one else had arrived. Where were they all?

A piercing cry in the distance popped their bubble of intimacy, as if to answer that very question. Not too far off, they could see someone approaching the church through the mud. They recognised one of their guests, injured by a fall, struggling to walk, covered in mud, worn-out, hurt, and helpless.

"We need to help him," the bride said to her groom with a worried look. She instinctively turned to race towards the guest. Unexpectedly, the groom took her hand, stopping her, pulling her in the opposite direction. He motioned toward an ornate, wooden door at the side of the church. With a puzzled look, the bride followed his lead.

The groom wasted no time. He hastened his steps. He opened the door, inviting her in. She entered and was overawed by what she saw: shelves filled with rows of boxes, hundreds, maybe thousands of personalised, hand-woven gifts for each guest, all named, but needing distribution.

"Will you help?" asked the groom.

"Nothing would give me greater pleasure. They'll *all* need a blanket," she replied, beginning to feel overwhelmed by the immensity of the project.

Again, the groom read her mind. "Just start with one," he instructed, handing her the box belonging to the injured man.

The bride took the box, stepped into the mud and began wading towards the guest, who was now struggling to remain upright.

As she walked through the mud, she discovered something incredible: her blanket was made from a material that was non-stick. As mud couldn't stick, no matter how deep she had to wade, the blanket remained clean.

When she reached the gentleman, she embraced him wholeheartedly and offered him his gift. He opened it in wonder and put his blanket on. Being offered something so precious and so personal made him teary.

"My friend," said the bride. "It's going to be ok."

He looked at his blanket wrapped around him. It was so bright and beautiful that it radiated like sunshine in stark contrast to the mud. He wiped his eyes and looked back at the path he had trodden, which had felt like a *very… long…* way. As he gazed back, he saw other people approaching of all ages, sizes, genders, and cultures - all guests - all wading through the mud.

The bride and the guest instinctively knew what needed to be done. At precisely the same time they said, "Let's help them!"

United in purpose, with the heart of wanting to help each guest reach the bridegroom, the bride and the guest planned to help those struggling through the mud. The bride went back to get more blankets. The guest went to support those who were walking.

Miraculously, the blanket gave them strength and determination to carry out their tasks with ease and efficiency. Because they were non-stick, the woven blankets enabled them to move through the mud so much more quickly. Oh. The effort and straining, how hard *that* had been! Now, they felt lighter, happier. They discovered their steps were firmer, more resolved. They realised they were stronger than they knew. They smiled at each other across the mud.

More and more guests arrived. Laughter and hugs abounded, as new guests put on their own, personalised, woven blankets. There was a collective sense of togetherness because they were all in the same sticky situation, trying to help one another wade through the muck.

The more guests that arrived, the more effectively they were able to help one another through the mud because they *collaborated*. Getting to the wedding was the goal. Coming alongside each other and sharing the load was the method.

They began to construct ways to make the journey to the church more efficient. There were plans of building bridges over the deep parts, and boardwalks over the shallower ones. They made warning signposts for pitfalls and dangers along the way. They became creative problem-solvers, finding camaraderie in working through the issues that presented themselves.

It seemed to be working out seamlessly.

But mud has a habit of getting messy, *very* quickly.

Yes, those muddy conditions were far from perfect. People began venting their frustrations about their mucky circumstances. People got tired, grumpy, and annoyed with each other. Some people imposed harsh methods of how to do things and got impatient when the outcomes weren't successful, or tasks were taking too long. People divided into groups and became increasingly exclusive as to whom they would allow to join. Some groups became territorial and would only help people who came into *their* area. Some groups refused to collaborate, even though they had the same mission and plenty of resources to share. Yes, at times, working in the mud made people stubborn, ungracious, and hurtful. After all, underneath their blankets they were still wearing muddy clothes.

Inevitably, disputes arose about how to best help people in the mud. Some disagreements were about methodology in muddy issues. Some were about who the bridegroom is and the kinds of guests he would invite. Some were about the roles they each had. Other times it was about leadership. They tried hard to solve these problems, but when disputes couldn't be resolved, some guests would go their separate ways and help people in other areas. Sadly, others gave up. That was the nature of working with people in muddy conditions.

To help, the bridegroom offered to teach the guests how to weave additional layers into their woven blankets, and to help patch relationships back together again. These layers included forgiveness, grace, acceptance, respect, inclusion, support, wisdom, and patience. He invited them to consider how to find loving ways of supporting one another in their sticky messes.

The bridegroom taught the guests how to create environments that were healthy and safe, where people could heal from the wounds they'd sustained whilst traipsing through the mud. These spaces gave people reprieve from trudging. They offered places where they could simply '*be*' and breathe. They provided areas of contemplation, so guests could consider how to look after themselves better in the process. They offered encouragement to keep working at their tasks whilst making wiser choices in their methods.

The bridegroom dedicated time to each guest, loving them in their own unique way, appreciating their contribution to solving muddy issues, and enabling them to find purposeful ways of not just getting through the mud, but learning to *thrive* in it. His words gave his guests confidence and grace, fresh ideas and genius solutions, motivation, stamina and, above all, hope. He kept reminding them that this wasn't the end, that what was to come would be more incredible than they ever dared to dream or imagine. His enthusiasm was contagious. His support was unfailing. His love was unending.

He kept reminding the guests of how much he appreciated every one of them by continuing to weave unique patterns into their stunningly crafted blankets, that they wore with gratitude. In wearing them, they knew they belonged with the bridegroom and his bride and that, one day, a celebration would come that would leave all this muddy muck as a dim memory...

Living in a muddy world brought the best, and the worst, out of people. They faced so many challenges that sometimes the complexity of the issues and the enormity of the task seemed overwhelming. How could they possibly find solutions in such a hopelessly muddy world? The murkiness impaired their judgement and decision-making, preventing solutions from ever being perfect. They had to learn to gracefully live with imperfection.

To assist with divisions and disputes, the bridegroom invited his guests to have facilitated discussions to collaboratively solve them, as best they could. It was never seamless, but that wasn't their primary objective. Finding compromises that helped *everyone* was. You see, when the bridegroom assisted these conversations, people began to look beyond their own interests to see what others might be needing and finding resolutions that would help *everyone* flourish.

The bridegroom shared his vision with his guests. He could see beyond the expansive wasteland of mud to all the possibilities that could be gained by working together *in* it. He could see how people could, in fact, *thrive* if they worked together. His vision was one of unity, seeing all his guests loving him and loving one another, whilst caring for themselves. He could see potential for connections to be made, even in the middle of disputes. He could envisage possibilities for people to grow in their unique skills, because they were invited to serve the common good. His perspective was so compelling that guests rallied around his call and dedicated their lives to making their world a better place.

Over time, some guests became builders and support workers. Some became weavers, teachers, and healers. There were visionaries who took a big picture view of the whole situation and administrators who worked out the fine details. Each person found his, her or their place to help one another in the mud. They committed themselves to the task, and to build unity in the process.

The bridegroom helped too, not only by giving them the tools and resources they needed, but he also set up a school to teach weaving, including how to teach weaving to others. Guests became students. He showed them how to weave intricate, personalised patterns and symbols into their blankets, making them even more beautiful.

As the guests practised wearing and weaving their blankets, they discovered joy in the process. They experienced moments of happiness when they could see people succeeding because of their contributions. Those moments made the whole process worthwhile because they knew – in their deepest heart of hearts – that love was the most beautiful choice, with the most transformational power, they could possibly make. To see someone's life transformed and improved because of the precious gift of love they offered, made all the effort totally worth it. One hundred percent.

So, they continued to work together through the mud with faith, hope, and love.

Their greatest hope was knowing they would one day enjoy the ultimate celebration with the bridegroom. On that day, ALL the mud would be gone. GONE! They would no longer have to struggle, strive, or be burdened by having to wade through it. There would be brand new, pristine wedding outfits for everyone. The old would be gone. The new would come. There would be no more pain or tears, no more divisions or obstacles, no more broken hearts, or fractured relationships. All would be restored. A new world would be formed filled with healing, restoration, and goodness, flooded with the bridegroom's abundant, endless, perfect love.

When that time comes, the mud will disappear
and be replaced with lush, green grass – FOREVER.

**What a glorious day that will be!**

# SUPPORT RESOURCES FOR THOSE WHO HAVE SUFFERED TRAUMA

If you need to speak with someone in relation to any trauma you have sustained, please reach out to a professional with experience in this area. Below are some suggestions and resources in Australia that you may find useful.

**Crisis Support & Suicide Prevention:**
https://www.lifeline.org.au/
https://www.suicidecallbackservice.org.au/

**Mental Health Support:**
https://www.beyondblue.org.au/

**Complex Trauma Support:**
https://blueknot.org.au/

If you feel like you're in the process of reconstructing your faith, and don't fit the conventional model of church, you may find this podcast useful:
https://www.spiritualmisfits.com.au

The following website is a registry of Australia and New Zealand based practitioners working with Religious Trauma. Their site includes resources and support material for those who have suffered from spiritual trauma.
https://www.thereligioustraumacollective.com

## ALSO BY JACQUELINE EAST

### Currently Available on Amazon

**The Leader's Roll** is an inspiring personal development guidebook providing useful tools, reflective activities, and engaging content to help you maintain your long-term leadership capacity by balancing self-leadership and giving to others. It is a self-paced learning experience that can maximise your potential.

**The Leader's Roll: Accelerator** is a condensed version of 'The Leader's Roll'. This book encapsulates the essence of the guidebook, but without all the reflective activities so you can accelerate the process. Lead others with purpose, integrity, and confidence, knowing your values, developing your strengths, and appreciating the uniqueness you bring to your community.

**ReCompass Your Imagination** is a beginning point for discovering the endless possibilities we can dream by tapping into our imaginations. It is written for anyone facing a significant life change and needs a place to start in building a new life. This is an invitation to open the observatory of your mind and explore.

If you have been inspired or encouraged by any of Jackie's books, **please leave a review**. It's a great way to help self-supporting authors have an even greater impact in the world.

## ABOUT THE AUTHOR

**Jacqueline East** is a coffee-loving writer
from Newcastle, Australia.

She has fun kayaking and playing with her puggle, Penny.

Jackie is a leader at Hamilton Baptist Church and enjoys creatively serving her church family through teaching, service planning, and event coordination.

Jackie has a background in education and is a qualified Life Coach. She enthusiastically inspires and motivates her clients to live wholeheartedly with authenticity. She finds fulfillment in supporting those in caring roles and leadership positions, helping them to practice self-leadership whilst serving others.

Jackie is passionate about Jesus and is dedicated to building flourishing, inclusive communities of faith.

If you'd like to contact Jackie, please visit
www.recompasscoaching.com
and send her a message on the contact page.

www.ingramcontent.com/pod-product-compliance
Lightning Source LLC
Chambersburg PA
CBHW032112090426
42743CB00007B/329